Memories

of

Kingston

upon Thames

The publishers would like to thank the following companies for their support in the production of this book

Main Sponsor
NPHB

Adams & Adams Limited

Broadhurst Heating

Eden Walk Shopping Centre

Kingston College

Kingston University

First published in Great Britain by True North Books Limited
England HX5 9AE
Telephone: 01422 377977
Copyright © True North Books Limited, 2000

ISBN 1 903204 24 0

Text, design and origination by True North Books Limited
Printed and bound by The Amadeus Press Limited

Memories

of

Kingston

upon Thames

Contents

Introduction

The Royal Borough of Kingston-upon-Thames is a name which conjures up many images in the minds of people who may never even have visited the town. Its association with royalty is perhaps the first thing which springs to mind. Films made in recent years retelling stories from the past which have been connected to the river around which the town has grown and which has been the reason for much of its prosperity, have brought greater understanding of a different way of going about everyday activities. For those of us not used to travelling on the water, there is a certain romantic attraction to taking a boat taxis to Hampton Court and to visitors of state arriving by way of the river.

But it is naturally mainly to the residents and frequent visitors to the town that Kingston means the most - those who have come to appreciate the many facets to its character, from the activity associated with its bustling shopping centres, night-life and the volume of the traffic in and around the area to the opportunities for pleasant riverside walks and strolls through the parks which are such wonderful amenities of the Borough. It is for those who know and love Kingston that we have produced this book. It is not a tourist information guide to what to do or see, nor a book of local history in the usual sense. To those familiar with its streets and environs there will, however be much printed here of great interest. We guess that the majority of pictures included here will fall within

The Coronation Stone was removed from outside Ye Olde Post House on 17 April 1935 to be moved to its present site alongside the Guildhall

the living memory of most of its readers, or at least not more than one generation from it.

For those who shop or work in Kingston but are relative newcomers to the place, there is a taste of what the town looked like in the not so distant past. For those who have lived in Kingston or in the thriving suburbs of Surbiton, Chessington, Hook or New Malden which surround it, there are plenty of

reminders of how things used to be when you were younger, you may even recognise yourself, a friend or relative on a photograph.

Town centres have undergone such enormous changes since the second world war that sometimes it's difficult to recall how things used to look, and Kingston is very typical of many in this respect. In this book you will be reminded that traffic used to go up

Children wrapped up warm to await the arrival of King George VI and Queen Elizabeth in October 1948

and down streets which have long been pedestrianised as well as of buildings which have been changed or even demolished over the recent times. It will provide a nostalgic memento for anyone born in the Borough but who has moved away for any reason.

We have enjoyed producing this book about such a fascinating place, which, through the many centuries of its history has been constantly able and willing to change successfully to meet the demands which have been placed upon it. This will certainly not be the final chapter as the future will inevitably bring further pressures for change and adaptation, which will produce its challenges to those with responsibility for such things to integrate reminders of every period in the Borough's long and distinguished history with the need for a place suitable for the requirements of the people who live, work and visit the Royal Borough.

Events & occasions

Above: 1950 was the year that saw the start of the war in Korea that still reverberates today. On the 22nd of May St John's Road in New Malden had it's own conflagration. At the end of the street was a dump for rubber. It caught fire and blazed for hours. It was three hours before the firemen could bring it under control. The thick black smoke billowed up to a column that reached 500feet at its height. It was reported that it could be seen 20 miles away. The smell must have been appalling, acrid and invasive. Rubber makes a particularly dense smoke and is difficult to douse. The residents must have tasted it for days. The people living in the street must have feared for their homes as the Fire appliances battled with the blaze. They must have been praying that the wind would not turn and bring the smoke in their direction. 60 Firemen in all were needed to fight the fire. Today there would have been television cameras recording the scene with experts warning of ecological damage and giving advice to the people of New Malden. This was before the Clean Air Act marked a growing movement against pollution but there must have been deep concerns about the wisdom of siting such a dump so near to homes.

These smart people are dressed up in their 'Sunday best' in honour of the opening of the Kingston Guildhall on 3rd July, 1935, by Princess Alice, the Countess of Athlone, making it another occasion that Kingston played host to royalty. These are the dignitaries of the town who have been allocated seats in the enclosure where the official ceremony took place. How fortunate those children were who had an even better view than those on the ground from their upstairs window, and how fitting that they should be in a property owned by

an opticians. Some of those not honoured by an invitation are standing around at the back; perhaps the uniformed gentleman on the extreme right was chauffeur to a family represented in the photo. The Guildhall building was an entirely new structure built on the site of Clattern House which along with the Town Hall had once been used for local government. The building which was the centre of attention on this particular day and has since provided the town skyline with one of its most distinctive features was designed by Maurice Webb.

From a high vantage point, the photographer has captured this scene showing the people of Kingston who had turned out in force on this bright sunny day in July, 1935 to witness the opening of their new Guildhall by Princess Alice, the Countess of Athlone who can be seen in the bottom left hand corner of the photo. Though they may have felt in celebratory mood, the people in the crowd are maintaining a respectful attitude to the civic dignitaries in the procession and a small number of uniformed officers were finding it easy to keep order. The original Guildhall was built soon after Edward IV granted the Charter making Kingston a borough in 1481. This was refurbished in 1706, remaining in use right up until 1838 when it was demolished - a new building was erected in 1840. The present building has a central tower which soars 122 feet into the air. The building on the left with the Tudor facade and bearing the date 1346 actually originated in the early 16th century and was known as the Crane Inn, at the time this picture was taken, it was popular as a restaurant and tea shop.

Both pages: In 1939 Britain's Prime Minister Neville Chamberlain had made his announcement to the waiting people of Britain that '...this country is at war with Germany.' The country rolled up its sleeves and prepared for the inevitable. This war would be different from other wars. This time planes had the ability to fly further and carry a heavier load, and air raids were fully expected. Air raid shelters were obviously going to be needed, and shelters were built.

By the time war was declared an army of volunteers of both sexes had already been recruited to form an Air Raid Protection service. At first ARP personnel were unpaid volunteers but when war broke out in September 1939 they became paid staff. It was their job

to patrol specified areas, making sure that no chinks of light broke the blackout restrictions, checking the safety of local residents, being alert for gas attacks, air raids and unexploded bombs. The exceptional work done by Air Raid Wardens in dealing with incendiaries, giving first aid to the injured, helping to rescue victims from their bombed-out properties, clearing away rubble, and a thousand and one other tasks became legendary; during the second world war nearly as many private citizens were killed as troops - and many of them were the gallant ARP wardens.

At the beginning of the war Sir Anthony Eden, Secretary of State for War, appealed in a radio broadcast for men between 17 and 65 to make up a new force, the Local Defence Volunteers, to guard vulnerable points from possible German attack. Within a very short time the first men were putting their names down. At first the new force had to improvise: there were no weapons to spare and men had to rely on sticks, shotguns handed in by local people, and on sheer determination. Weapons and uniforms did not become available for several months.

In July the Local Defence Volunteers was renamed the Home Guard, and by the following year were a force to be reckoned with. Television programmes such as 'Dad's Army' have unfortunately associated the Home Guard with comedy, but in fact they performed much important work. The Guard posted sentries to watch for possible aircraft or parachute landings at likely spots such as disused aerodromes, golf courses on the outskirts of towns, local parks and racecourses. They manned anti-aircraft rocket guns, liaised with other units and with regular troops, set up communications and organised balloon barrages. Other preparations were hastily made. Place names and other identifying marks were obliterated to confuse the enemy about exactly where they were. Notices went up everywhere giving good advice to citizens on a number of issues. 'Keep Mum - she's not so dumb' warned people to take care what kind of information they passed on, as the person they were speaking to could be an enemy.

Older people will remember how difficult it was to find certain items in the shops during the war; combs, soap, cosmetics, hairgrips, elastic, buttons, zips - all were virtually impossible to buy as factories that once produced these items had been turned over to war work. Stockings were in short supply, and resourceful women resorted to colouring their legs with gravy browning or with a mixture of sand and water. Beetroot juice was found to be a good substitute for lipstick. Clothes rationing was introduced in 1941, and everyone had 66 coupons per year. Eleven coupons would buy a dress, and sixteen were needed for a coat. The number of coupons was later reduced to 40 per person. People were required to save material where they could - ladies' hemlines went up considerably, and skirts were not allowed to have lots of pleats. Some found clever ways around the regulations by using materials that were not rationed. Blackout material could be embroidered and made into blouses or skirts, and dyed sugar sacks were turned into curtains.

Accompanied by civic dignitaries, King George VI and Queen Elizabeth make their way down Clarence Street on 27 October, 1948 to the spot beside the Guildhall where they viewed the Coronation Stone. The Stone is a weathered slab of grey sandstone which if given the chance could tell a tale or two about royal occasions, silver pennies minted in the reign of each of the rulers are set into the plinth. The last of the Anglo-Saxon kings crowned in Kingston was Ethelred II. Though not direct descendants of the seven Anglo-Saxon kings who were crowned near the Stone, this visit of 20th century royalty to the Borough nevertheless provided continuity for the tradition of royal associations with Kingston and its surrounding area. Queen Elizabeth has certainly had a special place in the hearts of the British people, and she has continued to draw crowds out on the streets to see her throughout her long life, just as she did on this day in 1948. Certain elements of her unique style of dress are apparent from this photograph, a hat sweeping up away from the face, adorned with feathers, a multiple string rope of pearls, a matching coat and dress and court shoes, and a smile indicating that she is genuinely pleased to be there.

The State limousine bearing the royal couple on their way to the opening of the new power station sweeps passed the site of Bentalls on Wood Street. The electricity industry had been nationalised just a few months before in April 1948. Today the massive Bentalls Centre has 600,000 sq ft of retail space and has been used by delighted shoppers since its opening in 1992. It forms the heart of the renowned shopping centre, and attracts thousands of visitors from Kingston and many miles around every year. Nearby is a giant store belonging to the John Lewis Partnership which was opened in 1989, a large multi-storey car-park for the convenience of

shoppers is nearby. But the wealth required to support such enormous retail outlets was still a future dream for the people gathering so enthusiastically on Wood Street in 1948. Perhaps none of the crowd would ever be able to afford the Rolls-Royce in which their majesties were travelling, but the first Morris Minor, a family saloon car had come off the production line on 8 October that very year and it was the star of the London Motor Show being held even as this Kingston crowd stood in the autumn sunshine. This model had a wider body than other family cars available at the time and offered better handling on corners; it had a 918cc engine and could deliver a dizzy 60mph.

Left: These girls are obviously very excited about the prospect of seeing the King and Queen. No doubt the event had received considerable advance publicity at home and for the older ones, school as well. Two or three of the older girls, with the panama hats which were so popular at the time are obviously wearing their school uniform, and may be doing so because this would have been their only warm coat, and in any case the anorak did not exist as an item of mass clothing at this time, however impossible that may seem to us now. The furry muff keeping the hands of the lady in the centre of the picture warm was just the thing for a chilly autumn day, when you were standing around waiting for something to happen - they were no use at all on any other occasion, but they did look so nice. It would no doubt have been a prized possession. All the waiting about on Clarence Street was on account of the royal pair coming to Kingston to open the new electric power station. There was increased demand for power, industry was returning to full production after the war and new domestic appliances were coming onto the market, revolutionising the lot of the housewife, the first transistor radio went on display in 1948 and in nearby Woking, Surrey Kenneth Wood was completing the design of his legendary Kenwood mixer.

Above: With Union Jacks at the ready, this rather gloomy collection of people is waiting for a glimpse of King George VI and his popular wife, Elizabeth. Perhaps they had arrived on the street early to get a good spot and were now tired and rather cold on this October day in 1948, at least two knitted balaclava helmets are in evidence as testimony to the temperature at the time. In fact standing has proved too much for one lady who, showing considerable foresight, has obviously come prepared with something to sit on, she can therefore not only take the weight off her own feet but also offer a bit of support to her young friend. They are nevertheless a very orderly group, very few having the temerity to even step off the kerb Royal visits were guaranteed to bring out a large section of any town in the days before mass ownership of television sets. At a time when we are all familiar with the appearance of famous people, it is hard to capture the sense of anticipation experienced by these people who may only have had a grainy newspaper photograph of the monarch to view before this. It was also a time when the monarchy was surrounded by a certain mystery which has disappeared, with mixed effects, in recent years. The lady wearing the fur coat at the extreme right, would have most likely provoked envy rather than hostility as she may well do today.

This would probably be a very colourful scene, but the black and white photograph requires us to imagine the colours of the blankets protecting these children from the cold on an October day in 1948. They are looking forward to seeing the King and Queen who were about to pass that way.

Something is causing a bit of excitement, perhaps they have caught sight of the Royal car. One or two blankets are covering the wheels of invalid chairs as these children had been given such a prominent vantage point because they were delicate in health or had physical handicaps. Some may have suffered in the polio

epidemic of 1947 when many children were paralysed and 700 of the 7,000 afflicted with the disease country-wide, lost their lives. Threat of this devastating disease was real and a permanent feature of childhood summers until a vaccine was developed by Salk and Sabin in the 1950s. Since that time mass routine vaccination programmes have meant that the disease has been virtually eradicated in this country. Two men at the back by the tree are intending to capture the scene on film, one has raised himself above the main body of the crowd but another has simply raised his camera above his head taking pot-luck with the view.

Left: A happy gathering waiting to see their King and Queen. They are all well clad with warm coats and many wear hats and gloves to keep the cold at bay on this October day. Those crates from Spitalfields market are coming in for an unaccustomed use. Look at the number of legs which are visible. If a comparable picture were taken today, the majority, if not all the women's legs would be covered by trousers, and the boys would be hiding their knees in their jeans. It was almost a rite of passage at this time, 1948, when a young lad wore his first pair of long trousers, not often before the age of eleven or twelve. This was as much to do with available clothing fabrics as with fashion - before the widespread availability of man-made fabrics like nylon and polyester, clothes made of woollen or cotton cloths were much more susceptible to tearing. Given the notoriety of boys to take every opportunity to climb trees and walls, the risk of tears was an ever-present one and though many housewives were skilled in the art of patching and mending, there were other domestic duties which claimed their attention and it was a task they wanted to keep to a minimum. Short trousers were sensible for another reason, before it became easy to wash clothes in the automatic washing machines we are so used to - boys knees are made from an eminently washable material.

Above: Eddie Calvert arrives at Fairfield Recreation Ground by helicopter on 24 October 1955. The police are out but not much trouble was anticipated; the police sergeant in the centre is spreading his arms to restrain the people behind him, but no one determined to surge forward, say to ask for an autograph, would be seriously hindered if they had a mind to step out of line. However, this form of rebellion was a product of later times and the picture shows a crowd content to take in the sight of the famous man from a respectful distance. This event, though not world-shattering, may well have been the highlight of a lifetime for the children pictured here - for this was a time when travel was less common and diversions of all kinds were far fewer than they are today, little did they imagine that their children would be surfing the internet, sending emails to their friends and playing computer games. Eddie Calvert, 'the man with the golden trumpet' was one of the top stars of the era, along with pianists Russ Conway and Winifred Atwell. Like them he had hits which went to number one in the charts, namely 'Oh mein Papa' and 'Cherry Pink'. The local press photographer will only be able to get a suitable shot of the star for the next edition if the man of the moment turns round to face him.

This surprisingly solemn-looking gathering is actually being held in honour of the Coronation of Queen Elizabeth II in June 1953. Perhaps everyone was disappointed that the original intention of holding the party outdoors couldn't go ahead due to bad weather. So here we have a Kingston 'street party'. It is being held in the church hall in the Kingston Hill area, in fact in Queen's Road at the south end of Richmond Park. Kingston residents rightly prize their easy access to this royal park. Since 1992 it has been designated by English Nature as a Site of Special Scientific Interest. It is also on English Heritage's Register as a Grade I site. Charles I enclosed it in 1637 for use as a hunting park, preserving the area as a deer park which it had been for centuries. Though it has been used in a variety of ways over the years, it still retains today something of its original character. The wide open spaces provide a wonderful amenity for the people who walk, jog and ride horses or bikes, as well as a suitable home to the 750 or so fallow and red deer which live there. A visit to the Isabella Plantation is always popular, especially in May when the rhododendrons and azaleas provide such a colourful display. A former place where deer hunters stayed, Pembroke Lodge, now serves anyone who cares to stop by for refreshments.

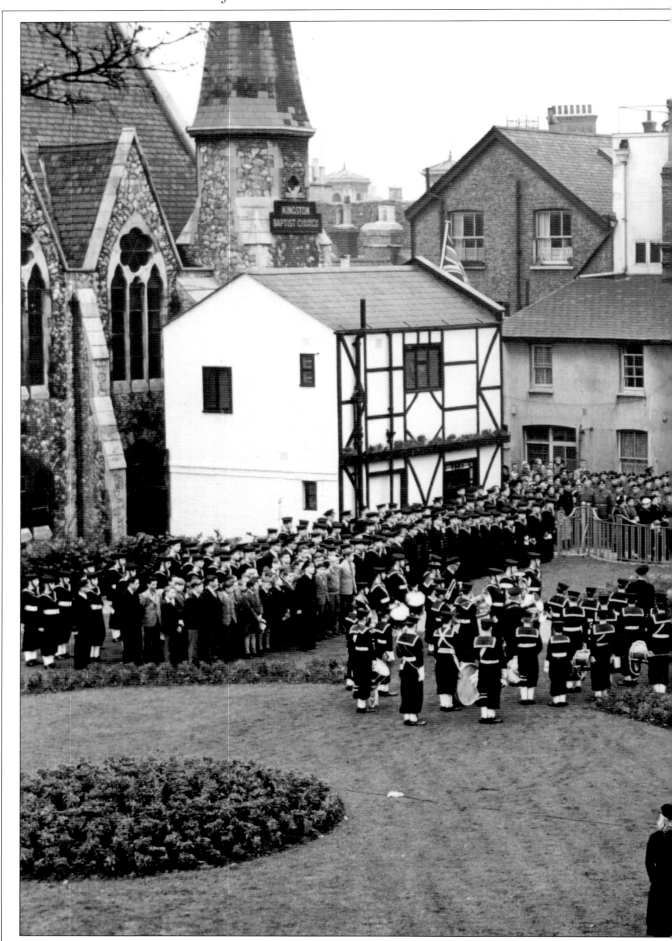

Remembrance Day Service, November 1953. This orderly and dignified assembly is taking place at the side of Kingston Baptist in Union Street which was built in 1864 in the neo-Gothic style so characteristic of the period. Of particular note about this memorial gathering is the sheer number of people attending, both as the representatives of the various uniformed organisations and in the crowd of people from the general public. This is not surprising given the date; there can scarcely be anyone present who had not personal experience of the human cost of war, in terms of sons, brothers or husbands killed or maimed in the numerous conflicts of the second world war.

Of course there would also be many who still carried with them precious memories of loved ones lost in the first world war. This must have been a really solemn occasion for those people and they must have had many apprehensions about what the future would hold, or perhaps they felt that things could only get better from now on. It is understandable, though perhaps rather sad, that the children of those standing would take the freedom gained by those they were remembering completely for granted. Next to the church stands the Old Mortuary. This had ceased to serve its original function and had been a baker's shop since the 1930s when an upper floor and the mock Tudor facade were added.

Left: What an apt place for the Coronation Party on June 2nd. 1953! It's Queen's Road in New Malden. The nation had mourned the death of King George VI in 1952 aged only 57. He died from lung cancer. He had not expected to be King as he was the younger brother of Edward who abdicated in 1936 to leave George and his Queen Consort, Elizabeth, to lead the country through the dark days of the War. He was well loved by the nation. His daughter, then 27, is now the second longest reigning monarch after Queen Victoria. The Coronation was a wonderful reason for everyone to celebrate. The hardships and shortages of the aftermath of the war were put aside as the young Queen rode in her ornate horse drawn coach to be crowned by the Archbishop of Canterbury. The few people who possessed a television invited family, friends and neighbours in to watch the ceremony on the tiny screens. Cinemas showed films of the occasion and children were given special souvenirs of the occasion. Street parties were held all over the country where everyone helped to make it a success. Meat paste sandwiches, jelly and fairy buns seem to be common memories. We wonder what memories the youngsters in the picture have of this day.

Above: Here is a sight worth turning out to see, a pageant requiring a fine day which they seem to have on this particular occasion. Here we see all the dignitaries from the local corporation in procession, passing the end of Eden Street. The front mace-bearer is leading the way to the Assize Courts, for the opening of a new Session. How many of the dignitaries pictured here were to be found earlier that morning polishing their shoes so as not to spoil the overall effect of sartorial elegance? The Assize Courts were built in 1811, next to Clattern House on the south side of the Market Place. The town gaol used to stand on the other side of the Assize Courts, but it was converted into a public baths, and later still, in 1897 became a public lavatory. Another public landmark of note in the town is the famous Coronation Stone which is at present near the historic Clattern Bridge, built in the 12th century over the River Hogsmill, close to the more recent Guildhall. A silver penny from the reign of each Saxon King to be crowned in Kingston is set into the plinth of this stone.

Below: Here we see the Lord Mayor and Lady Mayoress of the Royal Borough of Kingston on an official visit to the Elite cinema on 11 June 1951. The Mayoress seems pleased to have received this wonderful bouquet, which is very typical of the style at that time, as wedding photos from the period will show. The Mayor was there to rename the establishment the 'Century'; later it was known as the 'Century Elite' as the 'Century' name was not popular with film goers. Among the films on general release that year was 'Quo Vadis?', starring Robert Taylor and Deborah Kerr as the young lovers and Peter Ustinov as a convincingly deranged Emperor Nero and the epic adventure by John Huston, 'The African Queen' starring Humphrey Bogart and Katherine Hepburn. 1961 also saw two Broadway plays made the transition from stage to screen, Arthur Miller's 'Death of a Salesman' and Tennessee Williams' 'A Streetcar Named Desire'; this gave Marlon Brando the opportunity to recreate the role of the charismatic Stanley Kowalski that first made him famous in the theatre. Meanwhile British culture was celebrated in the Festival of Britain held on a reclaimed bomb-site in south London; Herbert Morrison, the Foreign Secretary at the time considered it was a good opportunity for Britain to give itself 'a pat on the back' after enduring the austerity of the war years and their aftermath.

Right: Dressed for this bright crisp day, a smiling Queen Elizabeth II walks down an impeccable line of Sea Cadets, who shared the privilege of forming the Guard of Honour for her with a detachment from the 6th Battalion East Surrey regiment of the Territorial Army. The date is 24 March, 1961 and she was on her way to perform the main part of her duties, which on this occasion was attending the 400th anniversary celebrations of the founding of Kingston Grammar School. This itself was on account of royal patronage, as the first Queen Elizabeth gave permission to the leaders of Kingston town to establish a free school there in 1561. The school is now well on its way to another century of progress and achievement. Kingston 'old boys' include Michael Frayn, novelist and playwright, Edward Gibbon, author of 'The Decline and Fall of the Roman Empire' and playwright R C Sheriff. The preparations for a royal visit exercise the talents of many people for many months beforehand, contingency arrangements have to be made to cater for all eventualities. Security has always been a paramount concern, though a discreet presence is always sought. Some people have been busy hanging Union Jacks along the royal procession route.

At leisure

This photograph taken at the junction of Richmond Road and London Road in August, 1954 shows what would have been regarded as a busy town scene at that time - somewhat different from what folk used to the situation prevailing at the beginning of the 21st century might consider busy. There is an interesting assortment of ways of getting from A to B, in the foreground a Rolls-Royce makes its stately way through the traffic lights, a trolley bus for those in a different income bracket, and not forgetting the pedestrians. The film showing at the Century cinema is 'The Wages of Fear', a 1953 production starring Yves Montard, a story about a manager of a Central American oilfield who was offering big money to drivers to use nitroglycerine in the jungle to put out an oil fire. Kingston has an important place in the history of the cinema, being the birthplace of one of the pioneers of cinematography, Eadweard Muybridge was born in Kingston in 1830. He gained an international reputation as a photographer before going on to develop a method of producing moving pictures - he developed the zoopraxiscope projector in 1879. Muybridge died in Kingston in 1904 and there is a permanent exhibition commemorating his life and work in Kingston Museum.

Above: This pristine, unmistakable 1930s art deco style, building was the impressive Odeon cinema on its opening day. The clean curved lines made a bold statement about the importance of the film industry at the time of the grand opening of this cinema in 1938 at Shannon Corner in New Malden. We wonder if anyone knows what was the first film that was shown there? A scrap metal dealer called Oscar Deutsch launched the film-distributing organisation in 1933. When names were being discussed Oscar put forward his initials and so the Odeon cinemas began. Shannon's corner owed its name to the Shannon Office Equipment Building. It is easy to imagine the status a night out at the pictures would have in the days of the heyday of the film industry when you see the building as it was. When Hollywood made stars. When children went to their special show on Saturday mornings and played at being their favourite character all week. It was thought that television and videos would be the death of the night out at the pictures, but we have found that they can all have a valid place in the entertainment industry. Too late for the Odeon. The building was later taken over by Decca Ltd. But has since been demolished.

This proud and happy group has gathered to celebrate the Kingstonian Football Club winning the Football Association Amateur Cup in 1933. The captain, holding the cup is F Macey, he could well have been one of the heroes of the in the bottom right hand corner. The Lord Mayor of the Borough standing adorned by his chains of office is Sir Alfred Woodgate. The team played in hooped shirts typical of many amateur sides, looking more like a school or university team.

Their is an interesting selection of headgear in evidence - the lady in the bottom left corner is sporting a characteristic cloche, the young lad has his school cap, while among the menfolk a top hat may been viewed at the back, but the majority are the fashionable fedoras, though a couple of cloth flat caps can also be seen. The main point of difference, however seems to concern a point of etiquette - should hats be worn or carried? Most favour the latter course of action.

Left: This is the Kingston Cricket Festival of 1953. Protective headgear was yet to be a necessity. The only people who were deemed to be enough at risk to warrant both leg pads and thick gloves were the wicket keepers. This was before the bowler was allowed to use today's aggressive techniques that were such a focus for discussion in later years. Nor was there a necessity to put such obvious sunscreen as is totally necessary today. Cricket matches went on for much longer then and there was a leisured and gentlemanly approach that was part of village and town life all over the country. The idea of playing in colours other than white would have appealed to many a housewife struggling with the dreaded grass stains, but it was unheard of. Whites were always worn. The players coming out to do battle had a good crowd to cheer them on, but the wicket keeper looks to have a less than friendly attitude to the cameraman, or woman. This was the year of a great triumph with England winning the Ashes from the touring Australian side. Denis Compton scored the winning runs to great acclaim. The Australian captain was Lindsay Hasset and the crowds were entertained by the skills of the legendary opening bowlers Ray Lindwall and Keith Miller. We wonder who was man of the match in Kingston?

Above: Who would have the job of the driver of this coach with the hopeless task of travelling down the street? He is transporting the triumphant Kingstonian Football Club, which is under siege from its loyal fans. The date is Sunday 23 April, 1933 and a sizeable percentage of the population of the town and its surrounding areas has turned out to share their jubilation at the club winning the Football Association Amateur Cup. The game which caused all this excitement in the Market Place was played against Stockton. The first game between the two sides at Dulwich Heath ended in a 1-1 draw, but the result of the replay at Bishop Auckland was 4-1 in Kingston's favour. This would have been a real highlight in the lives of those assembled here at this time - there was little else to celebrate. Britain in common with other countries was suffering from the Depression caused by the collapse of the American stock market in 1929 and it was in 1933 that Hitler became leader of Germany, though nobody outside the Guildhall on this particular day could have imagined what was to take place in the decade ahead. However, Franklin Roosevelt announced his New Deal in America shortly after he was elected President, and inspired hope once again in the hearts of the people.

There was an excellent turnout for the River Pageant in 1953 as part of the Coronation celebrations. The crowds reflect the great enthusiasm for activities on the river in those days. We are sure that the people were not seated as precariously as the photograph seems to show. One of Kingston's famous residents, the playwright, RC Herriff who wrote 'Journey's End' has ensured that his old school, Kingston Grammar School should continue the tradition of rowing by contributing funding. A regatta takes place every year but the population does not have the same enthusiasm more recently. As we find more time for leisure water sports and activities could again come to the fore. Visitors and locals alike can enjoy strolls along the riverbanks where there are boats to hire, public houses to visit and fine restaurants to dine in. Watching boats negotiate the locks, or walking in the parks that border the Thames on this stretch make for varied pleasant ways to relax. Kingston Bridge was originally made of wood but was rebuilt in stone in 1828 and is now reputedly the busiest of London's bridges. The river has been the main highway for Kingston until the railways. The station at Surbiton was actually called Kingston upon Railway. A world away from Kingston upon Thames. What may come next?

Above: All eyes are on the capsizing boat on the River Thames, and people are wondering what they can do to assist the people on board. The occasion is the River Carnival held on 12 September, 1964. The outcome was unfortunately a very sad one as a child was killed in the accident. The event was never held again. Nowadays it is the Henley Regatta which is so well known and which forms an essential part of the London Season for those with the leisure and bank balance to cope with its demands; however, there was an annual Royal Regatta held at Kingston long before the Henley event was started. Teddington Lock is just two miles from Kingston town centre, the Thames becomes tidal from this point. A family which has been associated with the river for about 250 years through its boat-building business is R J Turk & Sons. They offer boats for hire thereby giving visitors and residents the opportunity to experience the amenity of the river from a different perspective from that of walking on the riverside. There is now a member of the sixth generation of the Turk family running the family business. Jerome K Jerome, famous for his 'Three Men in a Boat' which follows the adventures of the friends and their dog up and down the Thames, knew the grandfather of the present owner and moored his boat at their yard.

Top: Kingston, with its three miles of the River Thames, celebrates with River Pageants as other towns do with street floats. As the photograph is dated 6th June 1953, it is logical to suppose that this pageant is part of the Coronation celebrations. The Beefeater costumes make a right royal impression. The River has always played a large part in the history of the town. Settlements were originally on riverbanks. It is thought that Julius Caesar crossed the Thames with his army here at Kingston in 54BC. Trade used the river for corn, coal and timber until the railways took over. The firm R J Turk and Sons has carried on its boat business for over 200 years and has recently made boats for James Bond films and for Stephen Spielberg. Tommy Sopwith first tested the famous Sopwith Seaplane here in 1914 In the 1920s and 1930s mixed bathing was all the rage from a raft in the middle of the river. Rowing has long been a most popular pastime in Britain and the remarkable oarsman, Stephen Redgrave has kept a boat in a yard on this stretch of the Thames. The British Olympic success in rowing is a reflection of the long-term interest in the sport.

Bird's eye view

This aerial view of the town comes from a postcard printed around 1920, produced to advertise the versatility of the 'modern' aeroplane. Kingston has played a vital part in the history of aircraft design and construction, being until comparatively recently a significant part of British Aerospace. The story began when aviator Harry Hawker joined forces with Tommy Sopwith, a plane maker and started to produce aircraft, including the legendary Sopwith Camel, before the outbreak of the first world war. It later became known as Hawker-Siddeley Aircraft Company Ltd and produced some of the most famous names in the history of military aircraft: the Hawker

Hurricane, the Sea Hawk and the Harrier Jump Jet all began their illustrious lives on the drawing boards of engineers working for the Kingston firm. But the cold winds of economic reality were blowing and British Aerospace found itself to have far too much capacity for its post Cold War order book and things could not go on as before. The imposing frontage of the Hawker building was such a feature of the area and it seems scarcely possible that something so amazingly solid-looking could prove to be a temporary structure, but so it was; the factory was closed and later demolished. There is now a new high quality housing estate on the site.

This aerial view of the town dates from 1938, the Elite cinema can be seen in the centre, one of a huge number of cinemas throughout Britain which were once packed with people from the immediate locality but which now have suffered from competition from other forms of entertainment. In recent years the trend has been for large cinema complexes with multiple screens to be built in places only accessible by car; people still go to these places to watch films but the experience of attending these centres is entirely different from that of the local 'flea pit'. There have been people living in Kingston for over 5,000 years. Excavations have shown there was a Bronze Age settlement here, as tools dating from that period have been found. It was the called the 'manor of kings' in the Anglo-Saxon period, when it was the place chosen for the coronation of seven kings; the stone used in the ceremony, the Coronation Stone, is still in existence and stands nowadays next to the Guildhall. The earliest written reference to Kingston was as long ago as 838 AD when someone called it 'that famous place which is called Cyningstun in the region of Surrey'. Its entry in the Domesday Book tells us it was 'the royal manor of Kingston' and that it had a church, (the church of All Saints which still stands in the Market Place), five mills and three salmon fisheries. The emblem of today's Royal Borough reflects this as it contains three salmon on a blue background. Kingston was a thriving market town during the Middle Ages. Later Queen Elizabeth I made a habit of hunting in the large neighbouring deerparks and in 1561 granted the town the right to establish a free school, Kingston Grammar School, which is still going strong.

This photograph of the famous Kingston Bridge was taken in 1933. All Saints Parish Church can be seen on the right. Kingston Bridge is one of the oldest across the river Thames and was the only one to be built above London Bridge until Putney Bridge was constructed. The original structure was of wood and built in the late 12th century. Tolls were collected from those wishing to cross it. In the reign of Mary Tudor, known better as 'Bloody Mary', Kingston Bridge was broken by the citizens of the town, loyal to the crown, so as to delay Sir Thomas Wyatt and those who supported him, who were seeking to prevent the marriage of Mary to King Philip of Spain.

Wyatt was delayed by only a few hours but suffered defeat shortly afterwards. As a reward King Philip and Queen Mary granted a charter to the town allowing a third fish weir and an additional fair, increasing the revenues to the town. The present bridge is of stone and replaced the earlier bridge in 1828, when the volume and the weight of traffic going across became too great for the narrow wooden bridge. The stone bridge was designed to accommodate 3,000 horse-drawn carriages a week. The people of that time could never have imagined the amount of traffic passing over the river every hour of the day every day now in their wildest dreams (or nightmares).

This aerial view showing St Peter's church on the right was taken in 1968. St Peter's was built in 1842. It stands next to the Liverpool Arms pub, which later became LJ's and later still was pulled down. Across the main road from them stands Rawlplug House, after the famous DIY product; this building was later renamed Clarendon House. Looking at the roofs of the different houses in the picture often gives clues as to the approximate year of construction. For centuries, houses were automatically provided with chimneys, as is the case for the majority in this photograph, however the flats in the bottom right hand corner betray their more recent design by their uninterrupted rooflines, which may be attributed to the popularity and convenience of electric fires and all types of central heating systems. Likewise, whereas every humble Victorian terrace house had a yard for hanging out the washing, residents of these flats, especially those on the first floor and above, would generally find it more convenient to dry their clothes on their balcony, when it was not in use for sunbathing. Today a substantial proportion of houses have satellite dishes on their external walls in addition to a terrestrial TV aerial on the roof.

This aerial photograph is looking east over of the central part of Kingston and was taken in September, 1953. From left to right you can see the Bentalls Centre, All Saints' Church and Market House. Kingston's location, close to the City and West End has always been a large contributing factor to its prosperity and its attraction as somewhere to live. The city centre offers the shopper a great deal from large and prestigious departmental stores to specialist retail outlets catering for the most exclusive tastes. There is a staggering 3.5 million sq.ft of retail shopping space, which makes Kingston the 7th largest retail centre in the UK, charging currently the 3rd highest rental levels. Today it is well placed for easy access to the motorway network, being only 8 miles from the M25 and within an easy distance of the M3, M4 and M40 motorways. Central London is accessible by train in under thirty minutes and over 50 bus routes provide regular services between all parts of the borough and other destinations in London and Surrey. There are excellent coach links to both Heathrow and Gatwick airports, Heathrow being a mere 40 minutes away. The nearest Underground stations are Wimbledon and Richmond.

This picture, from a old local postcard was taken looking towards the Market Place and shows a very calm and peaceful scene such as one is unlikely to encounter at any time during the day or night nowadays. The photograph was taken from a point near the Coronation Stone which stands by the Guildhall. The building in the foreground is Ye Olde Post House, formerly known as The Crane. Ambassadors and members of the royal court used to lodge here in the 17th century and at the time this was captured on film it was continuing its noble tradition of giving hospitality to travellers by serving meals and light refreshments in its restaurant and coffee shop. Its days were numbered however, and it was demolished in 1954, at 'only' 450 years, it was considered by those who had the duty to do so not to be 'old' enough to be preserved. How many Americans would find this remotely comprehensible?

Below: The Market Place, Kingston around 1930. This scene captured by J Dixon Scott shows the Shrubsole Memorial Fountain which was purchased by public subscription to honour Henry Shrubsole who had devoted much of his life to public affairs in the town and had used his influence and personal efforts to helping residents of Kingston. He was well respected in the town, and inspired affection also in those who knew him. He served the town as Mayor on no less than three occasions, and actually died during his last year of office in 1879, while giving gifts of tea to the poor. This fountain, to which many 'ordinary' townsfolk contributed small amounts of spare cash was unveiled in 1892. The fountain provided a valuable means of quenching ones thirst when in town - it would have been particularly appreciated by those who didn't have the money to attend one of the several cafes around the Market Place, and is therefore in keeping with the general tone of the great man's life. It is interesting to note that everyone is wearing a hat, a tradition which has died out almost completely since the end of the second world war. There was a time when you could tell what a person's occupation was from the type of headgear he/she wore. Nowadays, if anything is worn on the head, it's a case of baseball caps all round - often the 'wrong' way round.

Street scenes

Left: Watching over the disruption of the usual Market Place activities caused by the collapsed sewer in early 1956 is the Market House. This was built, in a spirit of great civic pride and confidence, in 1840 to a design by Charles Henman. It replaced a 16th century building that once held the Assize Courts. There has been a church on the site of All Saints Church, seen in the background, since Saxon times - the original outline of the building is marked by stones and can be seen outside the present south door. There is a conspicuous absence of those red and white cones without which life barely seems possible at the start of the 21st century. However the absence also of workmen endeavouring to remedy the situation is perhaps more serious, but at least it looks as if there are measures are in place to prevent further collapse of the road, though in a more highly safety conscious time, the precautions taken to prevent people falling down the two rather large holes in the ground seem somewhat inadequate. However, folk are just going about their normal business and, with the exception of the man in the centre, no one is paying any attention to the roadworks.

Above: This picture shows the view facing south down Eden Street probably sometime in the 1950s. The spire belongs to the Wesleyan Methodist Church, which in its heyday in the late 19th century was packed with worshippers. This time was known as The Great Awakening when Britain underwent what was in fact a revolution, but a beneficial one, in marked contrast to that which was occurring in France at this point. The original Methodists were noted for their very disciplined approach to life, in fact they were given their name because of their very methodical ways of going about things. Methodism was a denomination which came about by accident. John Wesley, having been ordained in the Church of England in his youth, came later to an understanding of the Christian faith which completely revolutionised his life; he sought to teach others about this in the Anglican church but found that the message was unwelcome and so took to preaching in the open air, often travelling many miles each day to reach towns and outlying communities. John's brother, Charles wrote some of the finest hymns in the English language, including 'And can it be' which tells about the new understanding he and John had come to. There is a long history of Nonconformity in Kingston beginning with Dr Edmund Staunton who was vicar of Kingston in the mid 17th century, this tradition was continued by two generations of the Mayo family, a father and son, who were both vicars in the town.

Above: Clarence Street circa 1932. The trolley buses are making their way down the street, no doubt whirring agreeably as they do so. The stately and gentle way these buses used to proceed is one reason that they are held in great affection still by many. Trolley buses used some of the overhead cabling used formerly by trams, they were linked to the electricity supply by a pantograph- sometimes this would spark and look quite dramatic as it did so. One or two cars are in evidence as well as a bicycle but the vast majority of journeys are being undertaken on foot. There is an advert for Craven A cigarettes on a hoarding, these almost unbelievably, used to use 'for your throat's sake' as a selling point. These were innocent days when people were not bombarded with information about all the health risks or benefits of various products and foodstuffs, as we are today, sometimes we can get conflicting advice within the same publication and often research contradicts the received wisdom of only a few years before. It is along time since hairdressers advertised themselves as 'saloons' as the Clarence establishment on the right is doing, and hairdressing itself has changed out of all recognition since this time.

Above right: Even for 1938 this must have been a quiet moment in Tolworth. A reflection of the last year of peace before the world was plunged again into war. Here at the junction of Ewell Street and Broadway there are no busy shoppers. The stillness of the streets and the van in the foreground, reminiscent of 'Dad's Army', could indicate early morning. The end of the last conflict had marked, in 1918, the first Labour Parliamentary Candidate for Tolworth, Mr. Thomas Dumper. The increase in road traffic gave rise to the need for the service station that took the place of the old farmhouse. Tolworth's night-life had recently taken an air of sophistication with one of the first Odeon Cinemas in the country when the weekly or even twice weekly trips to the Pictures became as much part of life then as television is now. It became the window on the world for the common man. One wonders how the citizens then would react if they could have glimpsed into the future to see the range of restaurants in Tolworth now serving dishes from around the world. People then might have a day at the seaside for their holiday. Whatever would they think to Chinese, Indian, Chinese and Italian food being sold in their local street? The world has come to them.

Below: It is early in the nineteen thirties in New Malden. The cloche hat and daringly short skirt are all the rage. Kingston has a special place in the history of film-making and in those days. the Plaza Cinema with its domed turret was an important part of the social life of the town. Members of the staff would dress up in costume according to the film if it were a big attraction. It all added to the thrill. They would feel part of the film, in small way. Times were hard for many people in the thirties but there was fun to be had. The fun was short lived at the Plaza as it burned down in 1936. I hope it was not when a film was showing. The site is now a MacDonald's fast food Restaurant. The delivery boy on his bicycle would be a regular at many homes. The grocers often had a boy to carry shopping to the customers. Telegrams would be delivered in the same way. Milk would be delivered by horse drawn cart. The broad pavement makes it a pleasant walk with the pram. The striped awnings were a feature of many shopping streets but they could be an inconvenience on narrow pavements.

Bottom: Here we are in the 'The Queen of Suburbs.' Surbiton. In 1958 we see Victoria Road busy with shoppers and the roads sporting quality cars. Is that a Triumph Roadster? The hoarding shows the durability of some brands. 'Heinz' and 'Walls' are still with us and are doing well. The overhead cables for trolleybuses show the need for public transport at that time. The cables were a commonplace sight in the cities and towns of Britain. Not everyone had cars. Trolleybuses made way for more and more cars and petrol and then diesel buses. Do people still remember the trolleybuses with nostalgia? Some towns have reinvested in trams. Will Surbiton follow this route? The station today has the most direct and so the fastest route to the centre of London so the commuter is well served. It's a short train journey to the delights of Hampton Court with its Great Hall and gardens enjoyed by Henry Eighth. Surbiton has maintained its range of exclusive shops, privately owned and highly specialised. It was an elegant place to shop in 1958 and it still is. Victoria Road has an interesting part to play in the history of the town as the first hospital began there, in a house, in 1870. It seems remarkable now to think of a hospital in such a building but the Victorians were rather good at innovation and the address seems appropriate.

Perhaps taking his life in his hands, in danger of being run over by an approaching motorcyclist, the photographer has captured this scene on a typical day in Eden Street August, 1954. Lichtenfell's quality clothing shop is on the left, next to the garage with the old-style petrol pumps which stand like white-helmeted sentries watching over the street. The odd bend in the road, from which the shot was taken, was made in an attempt to skirt the old water-course which could not be re-routed. This is an historic photograph as the construction of the Eden Walk Shopping Centre has changed this scene for ever. The shopping complex was started in the mid

1960s but was not fully completed until the final stage was finished in 1985. The cyclist in the centre of the shot felt confident enough to overtake the trolley bus - this required far less courage than a similar manoeuvre would today. He, unlike the motorcyclist, felt no need to protect his head with a helmet nor did he need a mask to filter out a high concentration of polluting exhaust fumes; the recent trend to provide designated cycle lanes and in some cases special cycle routes is contributing to improving the lot of cyclists up and down the country at present, and travelling in this way often means a shorter journey time than travelling by car.

Below: This is a view facing north up Malden Road, New Malden in 1961. The photograph shows a quiet moment on a road that was causing great concern as the traffic volume increased week by week. There was worrying congestion at peak times. The wide pavements kept a spacious air for the pedestrians but cars were becoming increasingly seen as a necessity rather than a luxury. The present volume of traffic would not have been dreamed of. There were plans to alter Malden Road to convert it to a pedestrian zone along the High Street but those plans came to nothing. The plans for a ring road also fell through, a disappointment to some at the time and a triumph for others, no doubt. There are two sides to an argument. The long-term result of the retreat of the planners has been that New Malden has retained many of its individual shops with their facades demonstrating the long history of the area, while still attracting new stores. Many people come to the town to enjoy the contrast to the congestion of other town centres. The village atmosphere has been maintained which is an intangible but refreshing aspect of the town. There have been changes, but they have evolved rather than being imposed and that has contributed to the unique feel of the town.

Right: A typical day on Clarence Street at the junction with London Road and an interesting assortment of means of getting around town. The Morris traveller, so much loved by their proud owners had distinctive wooden strips on the external door panels. Trolley bus services began in Kingston on 15 June 1931 but were gradually phased out at a later date when motor buses were in vogue. Nowadays the environmentally friendly method of operation of these buses fits in well with the spirit of the age, so concerned with 'green' issues, but the outlay for overhead cables would be too costly for them ever to gain serious consideration; however trams, once considered extremely old-fashioned are making a come-back in some areas for their efficiency in transporting large numbers of people through built-up areas with minimum damage to the air quality. This branch of C & A's, a company which was for so long a familiar sight in British High Streets, stands on the site of an old pottery. In an unexpected find, an old kiln as well as a large quantity of pots were found as recently as 1995. A cyclist and two people on a scooter, and not forgetting a couple of pedestrians, complete the picture.

his photograph shows Clarence Street in August 1954. This was a busy and popular route to Kingston Bridge which is now pedestrianised. Hayhills shoe shop can be seen on the left, and Lloyd's Bank on the right. The branch was built on the site of the King's Arms coaching inn. This was the era of genuine 'personal banking' when the bank manager was most likely someone who lived in the town and was known to the majority of the branch's customers. At that time it was possible to speak to him about your financial concerns in a way that is sadly becoming much rarer in these days of telecentres when even getting through to speak to a person and not a pre-recorded message telling you to 'press the star button on your phone pad' feels like quite an achievement. It also was not necessary to know your bank account number, the banks staff considered their job to have that information at their fingertips. There is an ABC ice cream van in the distance, the owner was doubtless hoping for a good day's takings on a sunny day like this. The shops on the south-facing side of the street have extended the awnings to protect their goods from the damaging effects of the bright summer sun.

Above: This trolley bus is going along Clarence Street in the early 1950s, something it was going to do for a few more years yet as the final trolley bus journey was not taken until May 1962. The tracks of the old trams which the trolley buses replaced are no longer on the street as they, along with other items of scrap metal, had been given to support the war effort. The subject of trams proved to be a thorny one in Kingston: the original horse drawn vehicles never appeared on the streets of the borough owing to strong opposition to their introduction. This sentiment delayed the purchase of the electric trams once they became available but when the matter was put to an open vote, those in favour were shown to be in the majority. An Etam shop can be seen on the right of the picture, a chain with numerous stores nation-wide, but on the left is Bentalls, a name with more particular associations with the town of Kingston. The business started out as a draper's shop in a small way, but over the years gradually increased both turnover and retail space, culminating, in 1992, in the opening of the magnificent four-storey Bentall Centre. At the heart of this is a 30 metre high vaulted atrium and the original shop facade which was inspired by Sir Christopher Wren's design for Hampton Court Palace.

Above (smaller picture): A photographer with a head for heights placed at the junction of Eden Street and Clarence Street, has preserved a picture of Mence Smith Household Stores for posterity. The posters in the white-washed windows are alerting customers to the fact that the business has transferred to the Empire Buildings, Richmond Road, opposite the bus station. It was taken looking down through the trolley bus wires in the early 1950s - a historic picture as this building has since been flattened and on the site is a fast-food shop. To the right of the picture is the Halifax Building Society. The 'Halifax' is still there but is now no longer the institution it was, having been demutualised towards the end of the 1990s and become a bank.

This photograph is looking down the length of Clarence Street from the junction with Eden Street. It was taken in 1962, just twelve years before the scene was changed dramatically when the construction of the Eden Walk shopping centre was begun. It was ventures like this which helped Kingston remain a popular town in which to shop when popular retailing went through an upheaval in the 1960s, the time when shopping changed from visiting individual stores to purchase items you needed and became more a purely leisure activity based in shopping villages grouped conveniently together in pleasant surroundings under one roof. Kingston boasts not only the Eden Walk Shopping Centre and Adam's Court but also the Bentall's centre which ensures that the town retains the coveted reputation of being the premier retail centre within the south east of England. The emphasis is on quality. with this in mind the Kingston Town Centre Management Partnership between the Borough Council and the major traders in the town was formed in 1996 with a view to increasing the attractiveness of the town centre to shoppers by ensuring that Kingston is a clean and safe place to shop. John Lewis built a new flagship store on the riverside in 1989 and Marks & Spencer invested in a major refurbishment of its store and opened a new one just across the road. In all Kingston boasts 3.5 million sq ft of retail space.

This picture was taken in the late 1950s and a marked increase in the volume of traffic can be observed. The pavements are very crowded and shoppers are sometimes forced to step dangerously into the road in order to move up or down the street. It was the increasing risks of this sort to pedes-

trians which led to the pedestrianisation of many main shopping streets in British towns; Kingston was no exception and banned all cars on this street in 1989, shopping became a less life-threatening experience as a result. This had significant implications for the flow of traffic as Clarence Street had until then been the main

route to Kingston Bridge. Kingston now has a one-way inner ring road system, which means that a wrong choice of lane can involve a lengthy, unintended circular tour of the town. The two-way procession of cars pictured here shows that in those days most British people bought British cars a trend which did not continue indefinitely as competition from other European countries as well as the Far East and the USA was gradually introduced. This was also the time when car companies were much smaller, in the days before 'streamlining', 'rationalisation of resources' and 'consolidation of operations' were part of the day-to-day vocabulary of business.

A **bove:** Clarence Street in May 1952 taken from the top of the Elite cinema which is now C & A, and an interesting selection of modes of transport carrying people or goods to Kingston centre or the surrounding suburbs. The most well-known of these is Surbiton which after having been a popular residential area for many years became a kind of celebrity as the setting for the enormously popular TV comedy series, 'The Good Life', starring Richard Briers, Felicity Kendall, Paul Eddington and Penelope Keith. However, Surbiton's reputation among those in the know is as an exclusive and specialist shopping centre as well as the place to find popular cafes and restaurants. The accent here is on quality and individuality. Such an ambience has earned Surbiton the title, 'Queen of the Suburbs'. It is also home to a number of chain store branches and the John Lewis Partnership opened a Waitrose store here in 1992. Apart from all the other attractions Surbiton offers its residents, it is the centre for an excellent commuter rail services into London, frequent and speedy trains carry travellers into Waterloo or Victoria stations in the capital. Chessington and Hook have both a good variety of food and general stores and are convenient for shopping by car; these are also very popular residential areas, offering their residents the benefit of close proximity to the countryside and the greenbelt around the Royal Borough of Kingston. One further claim to fame for Hook is that Enid Blyton whose books inspired at least two generations of children to read voraciously as they followed the adventures of the 'Famous Five' and 'Secret Seven' among other stories, was teaching in a Hook school when her first book was published.

Below: This is an alternative riverside development, envisaged by architectural students at Kingston College of Art. A proposed modern development for a site where timber wharves once flourished. Kingston was the transit point when timber from Surrey forests was transported to London. Some of it went to construct buildings of national significance. For example, in 1259 oak passed through Kingston en route to Westminster for the original Palace of Westminster. It was the scene also of the unloading of casks of choice wine imported form the sunny region of Bordeaux in the 13th and 14th centuries. Tanneries and potteries have also been familiar riverside buildings over the course of time. The view available to people on the bridge has changed enormously over the years, though how many crossing the river here can spare the time to take a look? The increased pressure of life has led to a different approach to areas such as riverbanks in recent times. Now the trend is to maximise the attractiveness of riverside locations making them into pleasant amenities for the enjoyment of folk wanting somewhere pleasant to eat a packed lunch in the summer time, or to exercise the dog or simply to stroll and watch the river flow by. Ratty from 'The Wind in the Willows' is not the only one to find rivers endlessly fascinating, many of Kingston's residents share his passion for the Thames.

Bottom: The Fountain Public House in 1949 overlooked an area that had so little traffic that it was possible to amble across with a coach built pram, a Silver Cross maybe? The child, born so soon after the War was one of the many 'Baby-boomers', now over fifty, part of the generation that has seen so many advances in technology. When the Band of Mercy erected the fine edifice in February 1894, complete with fountain, horse drawn traffic would have been the norm. Traffic would have had a gentler pace. By 1952 the motor traffic was posing a threat. The fountain was reinstated within the roundabout and can be seen there today. The land for the Police Station visible in the picture was bought in the late 1880s for the considerable sum of £500. The Station was eventually opened in 1892 when the Metropolitan Police Force was only 63 years old, as Sir Robert Peel had established the Force in 1829. In the distance we can see the overhead cables leading us down the road that has become New Malden's High Street. The lady striding away from us towards the road wearing the shorter length style that was partly a result of wartime austerity. Men and women wore hats as a matter of course. After a generation hats seem to be making a comeback.

Masters of all they survey

The firm which now trades under the name of Nightingale Page Hickman & Bishop began life in 1825 in Surbiton. This makes it the oldest established firm of surveyors in the area. Over the last 175 years the practice has changed both personnel and premises a number of times, giving them real life experience of working with people and evaluating property which is the basis of the service they offer.

Like all chartered surveyors, NPHB give advice on land, property, construction and the environment. Their expertise is available to private individuals, businesses and public bodies. The advice they are able to offer is needed at every stage of the 'Property Life-Cycle' and they play a key management role in the built and natural environment worldwide.
In the same way that doctors often specialise in a

certain field, so chartered surveyors build up areas of special competence and expertise. In the case of NPHB, doubtless owing to its long history, a wide range of specialisations is available to their clients. These include building surveying, residential and commercial property management and valuation, commercial rent reviews, rating, compulsory purchase and compensation, expert witness reports, surveys and valuations for home buyers, insurance reinstatements cost assessments, residential property valuations, residential property management and residential and commercial property sales and lettings.

Such a scope of activity bears witness to the complexity of modern life and current business practices but life used to be

*Above: George Frederick Page. **Below:** Claremont Road c 1920 (Kingston Heritage Centre).*

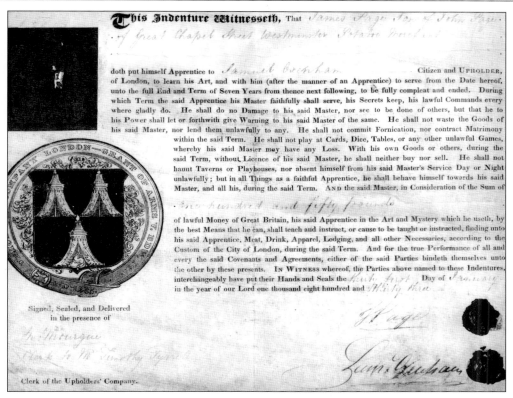

This Indenture Witnesseth, That *James Page Son of John Page of Great Chapel Street Westminster Potato merchant*

doth put himself Apprentice to *Samuel Beckham* Citizen and UPHOLDER, of London, to learn his Art, and with him (after the manner of an Apprentice) to serve from the Date hereof, unto the full End and Term of Seven Years from thence next following, to be fully compleat and ended. During which Term the said Apprentice his Master faithfully shall serve, his Secrets keep, his lawful Commands every where gladly do. He shall do no Damage to his said Master, nor see to be done of others, but that he to his Power shall let or forthwith give Warning to his said Master of the same. He shall not waste the Goods of his said Master, nor lend them unlawfully to any. He shall not commit Fornication, nor contract Matrimony within the said Term. He shall not play at Cards, Dice, Tables, or any other unlawful Games, whereby his said Master may have any Loss. With his own Goods or others, during the said Term, without Licence of his said Master, he shall neither buy nor sell. He shall not haunt Taverns or Playhouses, nor absent himself from his said Master's Service Day or Night unlawfully; but in all Things as a faithful Apprentice, he shall behave himself towards his said Master, and all his, during the said Term. AND the said Master, in Consideration of the Sum of *one hundred and fifty pounds* of lawful Money of Great Britain, his said Apprentice in the Art and Mystery which he useth, by the best Means that he can, shall teach and instruct, or cause to be taught or instructed, finding unto his said Apprentice, Meat, Drink, Apparel, Lodging and all other Necessaries, according to the Custom of the City of London, during the said Term. And for the true Performance of all and every the said Covenants and Agreements, either of the said Parties bindeth themselves unto the other by these presents. IN WITNESS whereof, the Parties above named to these Indentures, interchangeably have put their Hands and Seals the *Sixth first* Day of *January* in the year of our Lord one thousand eight hundred and *thirty three*

Signed, Sealed, and Delivered
in the presence of

Clerk of the Upholders' Company.

any loss.' The cost in terms of his personal liberty was therefore considerable and this was matched by the financial outlay required by his father - a hefty £150 0s 0d. For this the Master undertook 'by the best Means that he can ... to teach and instruct, or cause to be taught or instructed, finding unto his said Apprentice, Meat, Drink, Apparel, Lodging and all other Necessaries, according to the Custom of the City of London, during the said Term.'

much more simple and in fact most of the business in the early days was connected with agriculture, reflecting the main economic activity of the area at the time. From the start the firm ran the Kingston Cattle Market right up until it closed in the 1950s. Tracing the details of work the practice undertook throughout its long history provides a fascinating insight into the changing nature of work and society.

The document witnessing that 'James Page, son of John Page of Great Chapel Street, Westminster, Potato Merchant' was being apprenticed to Samuel Beckham 'citizen and Upholder [surveyor]' for the usual period of seven years stipulates the following conditions which, if required today may well cause much heart-searching, but more likely amusement, to anyone wishing to train as a Chartered Surveyor: [he should] 'his Master faithfully serve, his Secrets keep, his lawful Commands every where gladly do... He shall not commit Fornication, nor contract Matrimony within the said Term. He shall not play at Cards, Dice, Tables, or any other unlawful Games, whereby his said Master may have

The Estate Agents' Institute

Founded 1872

✳

This is to Certify that

George Frederick Page

was duly elected
a Member of this Institute

on

The Twenty Fifth day of January 1905

Jordan and Rogers, President
Arthur Strachett, Members
Frank Bristow, of Council.

Walter Jas Taylor, Secretary

One entry in the firm's records refers to J. Thrupp Nightingale's valuation of 'Towing path Grassland and Ponds' in the parish of West Molesey, County of Surrey. The extent of this land was 1 acre 0 rods and 30 perch. In it is found the following declaration, 'I the above named James Thrupp Nightingale do hereby solemnly and sincerely declare that I will faithfully and impartially and honestly according to the best of my skill and ability execute the duty of making the Valuation hereby referred to me'. In this case the valuation which was carried out in June 1873 was for £85 0s 0d.

Another page in the company records contains a valuation of the timber on the Fellcott Lane Estate, Hersham, Surrey carried out and signed by James Thrupp Nightingale, written no doubt in his own hand in beautiful and neat copper-

Above: George Frederick Page's election to the Estate Agent's Institute in January 1905.
Top: Articles and terms of employment of a young surveyor in 1836 signed by George Page.

plate handwriting. This valuation which was carried out on 'this 16th day of August, 1876' was for £15 18s 0d which included stamp duty of 1/-. Mr Nightingale was doubtless able to write fairly quickly but it is likely that a skilled keyboard operator could probably produce a many thousand word report in the time it took him to set out and produce this one sheet. Of course, which is the most pleasing to the eye is a matter of opinion.

It was after the first world war that the company started to handle a larger amount of business in the property market. One such trans-action was the auction of the freehold of 'Brook Farm', Hook Road in seven lots, which, the advertisement claims comprised 'Capital Building Sites, with considerable frontages to HOOK ROAD and to HERNE ROAD, DITTON HILL Ripe for immediate development'; the attractions offered by this land included 'THE SITUATION of the property is rapidly improving and becoming valuable for development, Gas, Main water and drainage are available. MOTOR 'BUSES pass the property to Kingston and Leatherhead and Surbiton Station with unrivalled service of trains is within one mile. Extensive Views are obtained from the property over a wide expanse of beautiful country.'

The firm spent many years actually in Kingston first in the High Street, then at the Eagle Chambers in Eden Street, and moving in 1976 to premises in Fife Road. Following a merger with another firm of surveyors, Hickman & Bishop, in 1994, which had been practising in the

area since the late 1930s, the company moved back to Surbiton, in fact to Queensborough House, Claremont Road just across the road from where Nightingale Philips & Page had started out 170 years before. The company has had many names over the years- it started out as Nightingale Philips & Page, becoming at various points Nightingale Page & Bennett, Debenhan Nightingale Page, Nightingale Page & Chancellors and presently Nightingale Page Hickman & Bishop.

Claremont Road itself has played a significant part in the history of Surbiton. It was the important transport route to and from Kingston and in the first phase of building of the area known as 'New Town'. The development was prompted by the coming of the railway in 1838 which linked the town to London. Surbiton became an upper middle class Victorian town over the next 50 years. The building of the road commenced in 1838 and was set around the communal landscaped Claremont Gardens. It has been designated one of Central Surbiton's five Conservation Areas in October 1988, which means that special consider-ation is given to all major demolition work; all works to trees; certain advertisements and signs; external alter-ations and extensions to existing properties; and all new buildings and structures. All in all this would appear to be the ideal environment for Chartered Surveyors to be located.

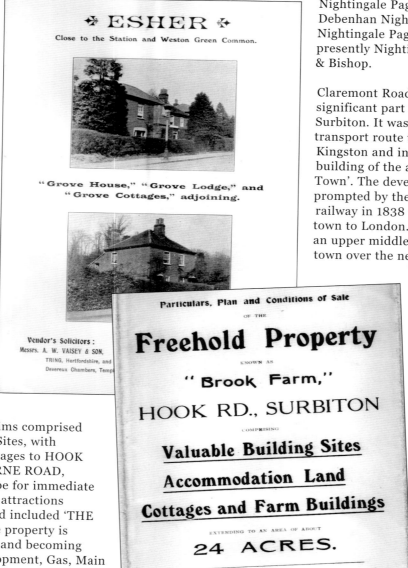

ESHER

Close to the Station and Weston Green Common.

"Grove House," "Grove Lodge," and "Grove Cottages," adjoining.

Vendor's Solicitors :
Messrs. A. W. VAISEY & SON,
TRING, Hertfordshire, and
Devereux Chambers, Temp

Particulars, Plan and Conditions of Sale

OF THE

Freehold Property

KNOWN AS

"Brook Farm,"

HOOK RD., SURBITON

COMPRISING

Valuable Building Sites

Accommodation Land

Cottages and Farm Buildings

EXTENDING TO AN AREA OF ABOUT

24 ACRES.

For Sale by Auction.

On Thursday, June 29th, 1922,

At the "SUN HOTEL," KINGSTON, at 6 o'clock.

Solicitors :
Messrs. DURHAM & CHARLTON,
13, Thames Street, Kingston-on-Thames.

Auctioneers :
Messrs. NIGHTINGALE, PAGE & BENNETT,
EAGLE CHAMBERS, KINGSTON-ON-THAMES.
And at Claremont House, Surbiton
(Opposite the Station).

'Phone Kingston 3356 & 3357.

Above: Two early auctions held by the firm.

Above: *Claremont Road in 1968.*

After 1855 Surbiton was independent of neighbouring Kingston upon Thames and remained so until 1965 when it was made part of the Royal Borough. Surbiton has always had the advantage of bordering the River Thames, stylish housing and better public transport services than many urban areas, and has a splendid heritage of buildings especially from Victorian and Edwardian times.

As the nineteenth century was coming to a close, the firm had taken out a lease on offices in Eagle Chambers, Kingston and interestingly acted as agents for the sale of the freehold when the owner, J B Boxall Esq passed away. A bill advertising the sale still in the company archives describes it as a 'Valuable Freehold Property, let and occupied as Suites of Offices and producing a Rental of £133 0s 0d per annum on lease and agreements'. The property was for sale by auction

which was held at the Griffin Hotel, Kingston 'On Thursday, the 17th day of MAY, 1900 at 5 o'clock punctually'.

> *Surbiton has always had the advantage of bordering the River Thames*

Owing to the length of time it has been practising in the locality it has had occasion to handle business in every street in Kingston and Surbiton. It has acted for all the major banks and building societies in the area. Today the focus remains round the same area but commissions from south London and the rest of Surrey are also undertaken.

Just as throughout its history the firm has contributed to the local community by providing services of the highest standards, so today the practice is committed to excellence in all it does. This has been recognised by the firm receiving ISO 9002 certification. Though one of the oldest practices in the UK NPHB has always kept abreast of the times, and now uses the latest innovations and information tools to assure quality and accuracy in today's fast-changing market environment.

A trolley bus driver and the conductor pose rather formally beside their place of work around 1932. The company which ran the services was London United and this photograph shows the trolley bus operating on the Twickenham route. London United was the first trolleybus operator in London, and trams started to be replaced by them in 1931. For many years the driver was separated from the main body of the bus and his sole function was to take the passengers to their destinations in safety, but eventually his (they were all men in those days) duties were extended considerably, conductors became redundant as bus design changed so that the driver could collect fares.

In the early years of the 20th century numerous transport companies existed to provide services to various locations in the area, but all that changed in the early 1930s when London Transport was born. This huge umbrella organisation became responsible for all road, rail and tram public transport in an area of 2,000 square miles around the capital. With this a corporate identity was born and the world famous red livery for buses was adopted. London Transport was also responsible for the introduction of the ubiquitous divided circle which adorns letterheads, bus stops, uniforms and the vehicles: a recent survey showed that this was one the most widely recognised logos world-wide.

On the move

Above: The Bus Station, Kingston pictured in 1925. This airy, and at this time largely empty structure, was built three years before by the London General Omnibus Company on the site of the gardens of Canbury Lodge. It was a central depot from which buses used to depart on the first run of the day to serve the surrounding community and transport its people to and from their various places of work and pleasure throughout the day and return to be cleaned and refilled with fuel at its close. Naturally the demands on services were greater during the working week which meant that there was usually quite a large number of buses 'resting' there at the weekends; it became, therefore, a favourite destination for schoolboy bus spotters who use to run the gauntlet of those in authority and venture to spot as many numbers as possible. This was a popular pastime for young lads especially in the era of the much-loved Routemasters which travelled routes into and out of the capital, so much so that every year a booklet which contained a listing of the entire London Transport fleet of buses alongside their numbers was published which enabled enthusiasts to mark off those they had seen and alert them to those they needed to make special efforts to view.

Perhaps an encouraging reminder that traffic jams are not exclusively a feature of modern life - here we have proof that they were a problem half a century ago. This is Clarence Street in February, 1956. Readers who remember how difficult it was to cross the road, or how long it took to get out of the town centre in a car or lorry may well appreciate the pedestrian precinct which now replaces this congested road. On the right is John Collier, which was, we were regularly informed through the adverts, 'the window to watch'. The Street was named after the Duchess of Clarence who visited the town in 1828. It was the considered opinion of Sir Clifton Robinson, the Chairman of

London United tramways that bringing trams into Clarence Street would turn the area into a major shopping centre - he was right. The town is well used to aristocratic, even royal visitors. Indeed Queen Victoria often came here and Edward VII spent a great deal of his leisure time here. Queen Mary, wife of George V made it practically a second home, and Thatched House Lodge in Richmond Park is presently home to the Queen's cousin, Princess Alexandra. The present Guildhall was opened by Princess Alice in 1935, and Queen Elizabeth II came to Kingston Grammar School in 1961 on the occasion of the 400th anniversary of the founding of the school by Queen Elizabeth I.

Bottom: The railway bridge on Malden Road in New Malden, pictured here in 1961, holds the key to the growth of Kingston. When the railway reached Kingston in 1838 the town began its transformation into a commuter link to the city of London. Rivers and canals were previously the highways for the movement of goods of all kinds. Thames barges could take heavy loads and great bulk, but slowly. Trains could transport the same goods much more quickly. Great horses were used to take the goods to and from the station unless there was a siding to the works or factory. By 1863 fifteen trains travelled daily to and from Waterloo. Kingston's population doubled, going from eight thousand to sixteen thousand in twenty years. It doubled. All those people needed housing and so Kingston grew. Dating houses pre and post the railway is an interesting exercise in New Malden as it retains its many links with the past.

It's a sunny day in the picture with a couple obviously happy together. The man standing by the expensive car. Is he waiting for someone from the train or has his friend failed to get off the bus? Will the double decker bus fit under the bridge? Is the van driver from the continent, or does he just like that side of the road?

Right: This trolley bus is passing under the railway bridge over the Kingston Road, New Malden in 1961. It was one of a doomed mode of transport as trolley buses started to be phased out in 1954 and the last one to operate in London did so in May 1968. The station at New Malden was opened in 1846, providing easier access to the rail network to local inhabitants who previously had travelled to Surbiton station - that was opened in 1838. Even today the rail service available from Surbiton is

impressive, providing frequent connections and the quickest and most direct route into London, thousands of commuters pass through the town everyday. The land around the station was developed by The National Freehold Land Society among others. What later became known as typical suburban estates were laid out bearing names such as Acacia Grove, Lime Grove, Chestnut Grove and Sycamore Grove. Today New Malden still retains a certain village atmosphere, and is popular with shoppers who wish to avoid the congestion in other town centres. Nor is the historical interest just comparatively recent, the church of St John the Baptist at Old Malden was founded in Norman times and Merton College was transferred to Oxford after starting out in Malden. Nearby Surbiton is the place to go for a good choice of cafes and restaurants in which you can relax after browsing round the numerous specialist and exclusive shops on offer there. There are also some chain stores to be found there, and Waitrose, the food division of the John Lewis Partnership are hoping to open in Surbiton in the near future.

winter. Nowadays awareness of the finite supplies of fossil fuel resources world-wide is promoting increased efforts to conserve energy and windows tend to be smaller and double glazed.

Top: Tolworth Broadway had become this busy shopping area in the late 1950s. Tolworth Lodge had lost arable and pasture land to give the wide roadway that is such a feature of the area. The road was sliced through the estate land. One wonders if there were protests then for the loss of good farming land, as there would have been now. The fine Shopping Parade housed many diverse local shops. This was the time when teenagers were beginning to wield their spending power. The record and fashion shops had appeared. It was a time of great change when young people felt that they could change the world. Saturdays had become shopping day. The photograph shows the lack of parking restrictions when car ownership was becoming common while most people still relied on public transport. The motorbike with sidecar was a common sight. Many cars still had the little indicators that popped out from the side of the car, more irritating when left stuck out inappropriately than a flashing light. Broadway has recently been updated into a dual carriageway and the area has had a facelift. The road that once split the farmland has now split the busy shopping areas at each side with underpasses to connect the two for the shoppers. It would be interesting to speculate what the next changes could be in another thirty or forty years.

Above: This is the view from Shannon's Corner, New Malden, in the 1950s. The company with this impressive manufacturing and administrative headquarters is Venner, founded in 1932, which made time switches. This building was demolished in 1976 to make way for a new shopping complex, consisting of furniture, pet and carpet stores as well as a supermarket. Burlington Road, in the foreground now lies in the shadow of a flyover which takes the busy A3 Kingston Bypass over this spot. How different a similar company location would look today - increased prosperity which came in the years following the end of the second world war is in evidence in the number of cars parked outside, but this is a small fraction of that to be expected today when two car households are commonplace and three or four cars in a family are not so rare. Large 'picture' windows were popular at this time, even though they could make rooms very hot in the summer and very cold in the

At the shops

Memories of **KINGSTON UPON THAMES**

The first recorded market in Kingston was in 1242 when the mediaeval street layout was being established. Charles I rewarded the loyalty of the town to his cause by forbidding any other market within seven miles. This still holds today although the market now is sited around Market House. Market day in 1948 is busy with people and cars, the quaint tiled roofs of the stalls adding to the feeling of continuity with the long history of the town. The tiled roofs have been replaced but market day is still an important part of life in Kingston. The fine statue that presides over the scene was built in 1879 in memory of the well-loved Mayor

Shrubsole who had three terms of office, actually dying in office while distributing gifts to the poor. The memorial was a water fountain with water troughs built in for horses and dogs. The Eighteenth Century Market house in the background was the original Town Hall. It is now home to the Tourist Information Centre and a coffee room. The Parish Church was built in the 12th Century but has been altered and renovated over the years. The wooden spire was struck by lightning in 'the great storm of 1455' and was rebuilt in 1505. The tower was rebuilt and strengthened in 1708 and makes an imposing backdrop for the scene.

Above: This attractive shop front is at the junction of Church Street with Union Street; Church Street connects Clarence Street with the Market Place. The shop belongs Mrs Louisa P Luxford, a fruiterer and by the look of things, a very successful one. Perhaps it was because she was successful that she was transferring the business to the Apple Market, putting the lease of this property up for sale. She may have needed extra space (or perhaps less space) for her produce or perhaps she felt the new location would be more convenient for customers, we may never know. What may be more certain is that she would be anxious to clear as much of her perishable stock so she had to transport as little as possible to her new business premises.

Certain things in the picture apart from the clothes of the people signal that it was taken some time ago - the baskets on the left are genuine wicker ones, and if the barrow outside the shop was more convenient way of displaying fruit than a means of transporting them, then the wooden hand cart would certainly have been in daily use, perhaps fetching fresh supplies of fruit from the railway station. The cobble stones on the right would almost certainly have been the original ones from the days when asphalt and tarmacadam were unknown. The two upper storeys would have afforded elegant and spacious living accommodation to anyone fortunate enough to be able to afford it. These premises are still being used for commercial purposes, though in a different line, the clothing retailer Monsoon has a branch there.

This picture of the Apple Market, off Eden Street was taken in 1959. The stall-holders seem to be doing brisk trade. There are stalls here even to this day, but the tiled roofs disappeared in the 1970s never to return. There is a great tradition of markets in Kingston, in fact the granting of royal permission for a market to be held was one of the chief reasons medieval towns assumed an importance which contributed to their growth and influence. In 1441 Henry VI granted the freedom to the town officials to control the range and quality of food for sale and to test weights and measures in an attempt to prevent the townspeople being cheated. By 1603 a regular Saturday market for cattle was in existence and a general food and produce market was established in 1662 under a charter granted by Charles II. In these days of supermarkets it is easy to lose the sense of the vital significance of fresh, good quality food being available within reasonable travelling distance. Diets were limited to what came in to the nearest market town and this in turn was dependent on what was in season at different times during the year. The possibility of strawberries in December would have been considered a joke.

T his attractive and intricate shop facade at 15-16 Market Place now belongs to the Next chain, but at the time this photograph was taken it was the home of Boots the Chemist. Carvings on buildings may be seen in many places in Kingston. The town has associations with many eras of the past. Of the only four Royal Boroughs in the country, Kingston is the oldest. It was the place where seven Anglo-Saxon kings were crowned, the first of these was Edward the Elder, son of Alfred the Great, the famous Coronation Stone at Clattern Bridge is a reminder of these times. There is also the possibility that Julius Caesar crossed the Thames at Kingston in 54BC in his campaign to put Britain under Roman domination. In the days when livestock was auctioned at the market, this took place on Thursdays, while Saturday was general market day. Today's market still retains some of its original flavour, and you can still buy produce and flowers there.

Below: This picture of the parade of shops on Malden Road, New Malden was taken around 1957 and shows a peaceful suburban scene and a wide variety of shops. On the right, Lewises was a specialist tobacconist, well-known in the area for the selection of exotic cigars, like Abdulla Cigars, which could be had for a price. Although Merton College, Oxford started in Malden before it transferred to its present location, this scene is more in keeping with its traditional and present associations in the minds of the local residents - it is a very popular place to shop and is a favourite with those who don't wish to face the crowds in Kingston on a normal shopping day. Most, if not all these shops would have been owned and run by members of the proprietor's family. Customers were known by name and shoppers expected to spend quite a long time doing their shopping, as there was always time to catch up on the local news and enquire about the health of people one met. How

different from today when High Streets wherever you go look almost identical and big chains of fast-food, stationery and video shops seem to dominate the scene.

Bottom: A chance to purchase bargains at a well-known Kingston shop is on offer for a limited period only. Mackney's drapery store which supplied countless items of household linens over the years was having its closing down sale. Fife Road which was where the shop had traded for many a year was an important shopping area at the end of the 1950s when this picture was taken, but it had not always been so. Until the mid 19th century market gardens were situated off this road, but the land was gradually taken over for building. It became the home of the Royal County Theatre in 1897, which in the course of time became Super Cinema, the first in the area to show talkies. It was gutted in 1949. Kingston has a number of associations with some famous names of stage and screen. Lilley Langtrey lived on Kingston Hill, though it must be said that she is most famous not as an actress but for the fact that she was mistress to Edward VII. Margaret Lockwood, who starred in the Hollywood film, 'The Wicked Lady' chose Kingston as her residence for the last thirty years of her life. Michael Frayn, known as the writer of 'Noises Off' and as distinguished novelist, journalist and translator attended Kingston Grammar School, as did Edward Gibbon, author of 'Decline and Fall of the Roman Empire' and R C Sheriff who wrote the play, 'Journey's End'.

Making a living

A **bove:** A photograph taken in 1942, showing the men at R B Page & Co at the factory at the Bittoms hard at work producing aircraft parts. This was a vital occupation at this time during the second world war. This firm made an important contribution to the aircraft industry which is better known for the business established by Tommy Sopwith and Harry Hawker, which for many years was a major employer in the town. This was an exciting time in the world of aviation, and not only in the field of military aircraft, the first pressurised airliner, the Boeing Stratoliner, had made its maiden flight less than three years before this picture was taken, and British Airways was formed by the merger of Hillman, Spartan and United Airways. 1942 saw the emergence of an item of clothing which we regard as indispensable. A new 'T-type' shirt was produced for the US Navy, such garments had been known before this but only as underwear, now it made the switch to outerwear and has since proved extremely popular.

In the picture the Coronation Stone is being removed from outside Ye Olde Post House on the 17th April 1935 to be moved to its present site alongside the Guildhall. The Stone is a remarkable link with Kingston's association with Royalty. It was used in the ceremonies when seven Saxon kings were crowned in the town during the 10th Century. A silver penny from the reign of each of the monarchs is set into the plinth of the stone. The Stone was rescued from obscurity in 1850; it did not later have the same sad end as the historic Post House that had served as a military headquarters for Cromwell only to become a restaurant in 1912 and then to be demolished in 1954. It was certainly a building of great charm in 1935, with its row of shops including a curiosity shop. The optician sign is a fine example of the shop signs of the day. The horse drawn cart used by the artisans give a real flavour of the pre-war times when horses were commonly used. The impression is that the workman who is standing is the senior stonemason. The stone is now set on a concrete platform over the River Hogsmill by the 12th Century Clattern Bridge where Princess Alice opened the present Guildhall in 1935.

This photograph was taken on 19 October, 1948, the day this giant twin-chimneyed edifice was opened, on the bank of the Thames. Ever controversial as far as local residents were concerned, the electricity power station, though huge was never, in fact big enough for its intended purpose.

Electricity generation from fossil fuels declined in the latter part of the 20th century, being replaced by the increased use of nuclear fuel. This station was closed in 1980 and the chimneys, a notable landmark for so long were blown up in the early 1990s. The plant was built on a site previously occupied by a sewage works called

Native Guano Co., this was a company with a world-wide reputation - however, locally is was primarily known for being rather smelly. Other sections of the Thames are much more attractive, including stretches along which there are many pubs and restaurants which provide an agreeable destination for a leisurely boat trip. A large choice of river craft are available for hire and during the summer months many enjoy a boat trip to Hampton Court or Richmond. For those wishing to keep their feet firmly on dry land, a walk along the riverside can be a very pleasant way of passing an hour or two in the open air.

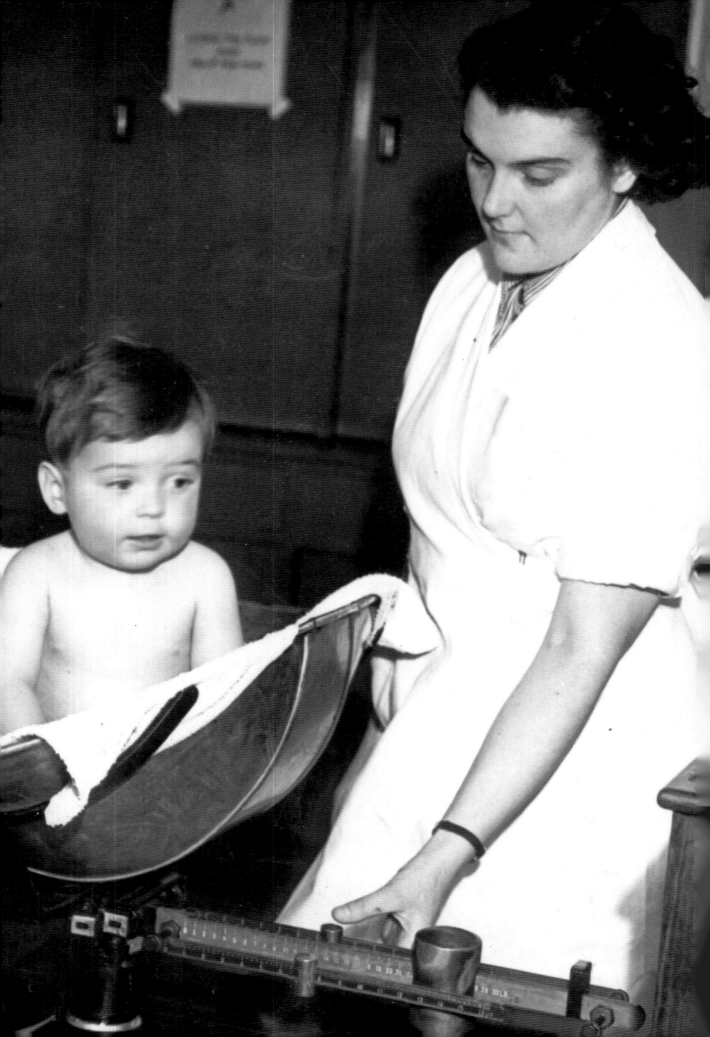

Both pages: It was possibly the acute wartime shortages of food and supplies which made doctors, health workers and mothers alike very aware of the health of the new generation, and children were carefully weighed, measured and immunised against the illnesses that had at one time meant disfigurement or even death *(facing page)*. A vaccine for polio, the scourge of former years which left behind its terrible mark of wasted and useless limbs, only came later, however. American scientist Jonas Edward Salk developed a vaccine in 1955, and an oral vaccine was produced in 1960. The vaccines brought the dreaded disease under control and today polio is rarely seen. On

a day to day basis, vitamins were vital to the health of children, and long before the advent of the cod liver oil capsule, the recommended spoonful of cod liver oil was administered to the youngest children every day in schools and nurseries around the country during the 1940s. Children might have screwed up their noses at the fishy taste, but the nourishing cod liver oil went a long way towards keeping them healthy. The vitamin-packed orange juice was far more palatable, and artful mothers would often use the orange juice as a bribe: no cod liver oil, no orange juice. Following hard on the heels of the oil, the juice took away the distinctive taste that was disliked by so many children. Ante-natal clinics

did all they could to check on the diet, blood pressure and vitamin intake of mothers to be; our carefully posed photograph, taken in an ante-natal clinic in the 1930s, records at least the cleanliness and tidiness that was to their great credit *(bottom)*. And when the tiny new citizen finally arrived, there were health visitors to pay friendly calls on families in their homes to check on the health and happiness of mothers and babies *(left)*. National Dried Milk for babies was also made available to mothers, and before today's push towards natural feeding NDM was for decades very much in vogue. We need to remember that at the time of these photographs the National Health service did not exist, and in fact the NHS only came into operation after World War II in July 1948.

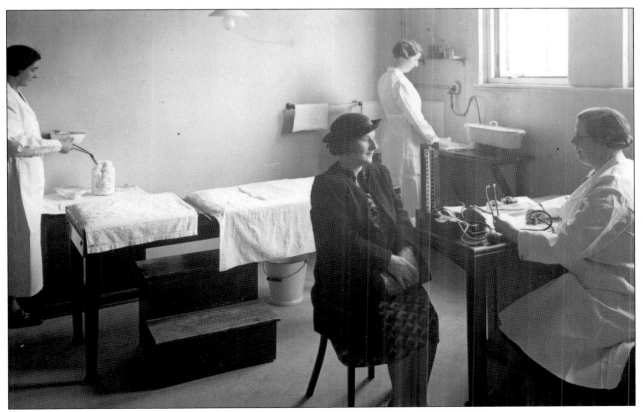

Above: How many of these construction workers from Surrey Construction company have been 'beefed up' on the Fray Bentos corned beef advertised on the hoarding on the left? They are undertaking the reconstruction of the railway bridge over the Richmond Road in 1958. The railway was a relatively late comer to Kingston, perhaps on account of its importance as a coaching town, and the benefit its residents had of travelling by river. In the 18th century the Kingston Hill area was the notorious hideout of highwaymen who took advantage of the extreme vulnerability of those hazarding the dangers of travel at the time, and under the threat of death relieved passengers of any ready cash and valuables they had, thereby keeping themselves in the luxury to which they became easily accustomed. Trains did not appear in Kingston until 1863, when a branch on the Twickenham to Windsor line opened in July 1863. This was added to six years later when the 'Kingston Loop' provided a means of getting to Wimbledon via Malden. The coming of the railway resulted in the rapid expansion of the population; service industries as well as light industrial concerns were established, and the wealth which these generated supported numerous shops which were the foundation for the strength of Kingston as a major retail centre today.

Below centre: In the centre in the distance this photograph shows the distinctive 'pyramid roof' of the Guildhall, which was opened by Princess Alice in 1935. In the foreground the rebuilding of the Two Brewers pub is well underway. The year is 1956, the place Wood Street. A new mood of optimism was emerging in Britain at this time. Rationing had ended two years before and people were looking forward to better days ahead. The Dream Weavers were telling everybody that 'It's almost tomorrow' and cinema goers feasted their eyes on the opulence found in the court of the King of Siam in the lavish adaptation of Rodgers and Hammerstein's 'The King and I' starring Deborah Kerr and Yul Brynner. The pub was demolished at the turn of the new century. In the 18th century the Horsefair district of the town had a licensed house for every 37 people. The Beerhouse Act, passed in 1830 actually worsened the situation as it permitted anyone with his name on the rate book to open a beer shop. The church in the picture is All Saints, the Parish church of Kingston. This is a Grade I listed building, originally built in the 12th century and restored and extended in the mid 19th century, under the influence of the religious revival from the impetus of the Oxford Movement.

Lifelong learning at Kingston College

The history of Kingston College is to be found in the industrial ambition of Britain in the late 19th century to match the challenge of growing competitors such as Germany and the USA. By the early 1880s classes for young men were being held in National School premises in Wood Street under the co-ordination of the Kingston Young Men's Club and Institute. In 1892 the Kingston Technical Instruction Committee was formed, one of whose main concerns was accommodation. In 1894 Inspectors of Science and Art Schools declared themselves satisfied with the teaching "despite teachers' and students' present disadvantageous surroundings". Electricity, Plumbing, Carpentry, Chemistry, Dressmaking, Cookery, French and German featured on the programme.

Long negotiations with Surrey County Council resulted in approval being given for the construction of new premises in Kingston Hall Road. The distinctive red brick building was

Above: *An early prospectus.*
Below: *The original building.*

V. R.

KINGSTON
SCIENCE AND ART
EVENING CLASSES,

In connection with the Science and Art Department, South Kensington.

Committee:—Mr. B. MARSH (Chairman), Rev. A. S. W. YOUNG, Mr. R. SEELEY, Mr. A. FISHER, Dr. BIDDLE, Mr. W. WALTERS, Mr. H. RYMER, Dr. WOOLLEY, Rev. J. M. GORDON.
Mr. J. HIDE, Secretary.

The Classes will be re-opened for the

Fourth Session, 1878-9,
AT
THE SCHOOL ROOMS, WOOD STREET,
THE FIRST WEEK IN OCTOBER.

SUBJECTS:

ART.	SCIENCE.
Freehand Drawing.	Solid Geometry.
Geometrical Drawing.	Building Construction.
Model Drawing.	Physiology or Physiography.
Perspective Drawing.	Chemistry.
Landscape Ink & Sepia Drawing.	Acoustics, Light and Heat.
Drawing from Casts.	Magnetism and Electricity.

N.B.—The Science Classes will be formed if a sufficient number of Students send in their names by the First Week in October.

Members of these Classes are eligible to compete for Queen's Prizes and Certificates, Science, Art, and Whitworth Scholarships, and Local Prizes.

Full information may be obtained from Mr. W. H. WEBB, National Schools, Wood-street, Kingston-on-Thames, or 1, Laurel-villas, King Charles'-road, Surbiton, to whom application should be made for admission to Classes.

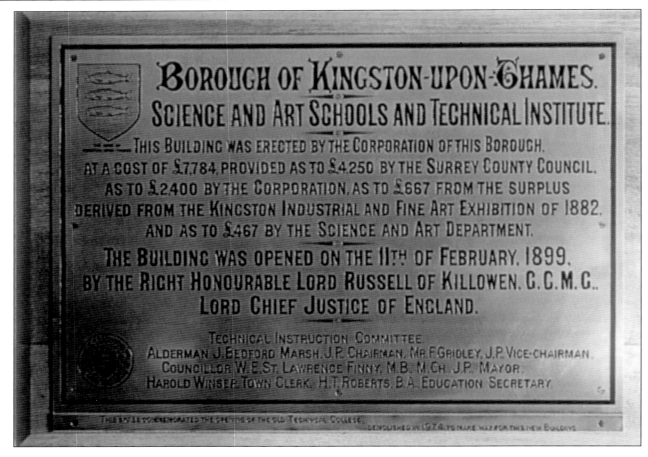

opened on 11th February, 1899 and graced the town until its demolition in 1971. The event was marked by the presence of Lord Russell, Lord Chief Justice at the time. The reporter from the Surrey Comet became enthralled with the plumbing exhibits: 'the pipe bending, notably the double turns made with two inch and four inch pipe, were excellent.'

No sooner was this considerable project completed than expansion again had to be considered. In 1902 a new wing was built. Classes in Telegraphy, Book-Keeping, Botany, Hygiene and Workshop Arithmetic began. Balfour's Education Act of 1902 facilitated a huge expansion in Secondary Education, and Kingston was not slow in taking advantage of this development. In 1911 Surrey County Council approved the construction of a further extension at the rear of the Institute. The first world war curtailed plans for more expansion, but 1,459 volunteers enrolled on courses in Ambulance, Nursing and Invalid Cookery, as well as Aero-engineering and Aeroplane Design.

The inter-war years saw a steady expansion with gradual diversification of courses, including Agriculture, Psychology for Teachers and even Esperanto! By 1939 3,388 students were entered for public examinations compared with 1,350 in 1935. The average salary of a College Instructor was nine shillings per hour. The last major change of the 1930s came abut in 1939 when a spacious building was completed in Knight's Park to house the new full-time School of Art.

Above: *The college's foundation plaque.*
Right: *Dominic Bruce, the first Principal of KCFE.*

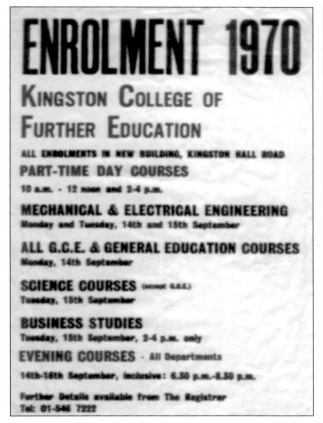

Diploma, although links between the two institutions always remained strong.

KCFE made rapid strides in the 1960s, student enrolments increasing from 3,968 to 5,048, but the next decade proved to be much more difficult. Four stages of expansion were foreseen, involving the demolition of the old Victorian block. The eleven-storey tower block of stage two was completed and plans for stage three lay on the drawing board, when the government intervened with the dreaded 'cuts'. Not until 1984 did work start at the St James's Road end of the main site. When KCFE became a self governing institution in 1993 stage four could be contemplated, work being commenced in 1999.

The second world war inevitably brought new demands, with air raid sirens disrupting classes and courses being established to cope with the needs of wartime, as had happened 25 years earlier.

An overwhelming demand for further education in the post-war years led to significant increases in full-time classes once again, creating a need for extra accommodation. The College's Golden Jubilee Year began with plans for additional premises in Kingston Hall Road which were realised in the following year, and new Engineering workshops were ready for business in 1950.

Golden Jubilee celebrations began with plans for additional premises in Kingston Hall Road

However, buildings alone do not make a successful place to study. The history of Kingston College is testimony to what can be achieved with quite often inadequate resources. In 1996-7 some 3,600 full-time and 3,400 part-time students enrolled. Kingston College has successfully weathered the storms of the 70s, 80s and 90s, with the range of courses ever-widening.

As the decade progressed Britain was again responding to fears about competition from abroad, notably Russia and America. This was the era of the sputnik and the space race. Accordingly, Surrey County Council decided in 1961 to divide Kingston Technical College into Kingston College of Technology (now Kingston University) and Kingston College of Further Education, now renamed Kingston College. The latter concentrated on academic and vocational education up to GCE 'A' Level and Ordinary National

The new millennium should see a dramatic programme of building development that will enhance still further the College's reputation for excellence in education and training.

Top left: *The 1970 enrolment advertisement.*
Top right: *A celebration of a college founded on 'whisky money'.* **Right:** *Arthur Cotterell, Principal since 1984.*

Broadhurst Heating - hot news for Kingston

It doesn't seem so long ago that winters were a time of icy blasts and freezing drafts... and out of doors was even worse! Most of us recall the days before central heating became the norm. Then as winter struck we would huddle round our coal fires, or if we were a little luckier around the gas fires or electric heaters in that small part of our homes which was truly warm listening to our older relatives complaining about a draft coming from somewhere. 'Shut that door' wasn't a catch phrase we picked up from Larry Grayson on the telly but something we heard people say every day as heat flooded out of the room and cold air swept in. Even indoors it

was normal to wear at least three layers of clothing: vests, shirts and jumpers for boys or blouses and cardigans for girls. Men seldom removed their jackets and wearing a hat in the house was not uncommon.

What we needed, did we but know it, was central heating. Not that many had central heating back then, but some did. One of the first firms to begin installing heating systems in a big way was the Surbiton firm of Broadhurst Heating Ltd.

thought Britain a rather poor posting after having been raised in the sunnier climes of Italy. But not to worry, they had the answer. Remains of Roman central heating systems can be found in sites all over Britain with the spaces under floors and between walls designed in such a way that hot air from a furnace could circulate around the chosen rooms providing a warm environment even in the worst of the British weather. Sadly for fifteen hundred years after the departure of the Romans we poor British had to contend with fighting off the cold with log and coal fires in our

Not that the firm was the first. The Romans were actually the first to bring the joys of central heating to the British Isles. The poor Romans must have

Above (both pictures): *The Guild Hall and boiler room.*

miserable homes until the arrival of relatively modern times. In the 1950s and 60s greater prosperity following the ending of the second world war led to an increasing demand for a better way of heating our homes, schools, factories and shops. And one plumber in particular was keen to lead the way.

The Broadhurst heating business was founded in November 1957 by Brian John Broadhurst; from the age of 16 he had worked as a plumber for Moss & Pizzey, plumbers in Chessington. He worked for Moss & Pizzey both before an after his army service. Between 1951 and 1953 Brian Broadhurst had done two years national service spending much of the time in Egypt - perhaps that is where he acquired his abiding interest in keeping warm!

Whilst working for Moss & Pizzey, Brian was lent out to the heating company, SS Leach, where he soon realised that heating was the coming thing.

Like many keen young men before him Brian worked for employers until six and then worked from home for himself until 10 or 11pm in the evening getting his first two jobs on his own account in Edgware and in Mill Hill. It cannot have been easy but he was clearly a young man with plenty of energy and a strong desire to get on in the world.

In 1957 Brian Broadhurst decided to set up on his own and concentrate on heating rather than plumbing. His fledgling firm became one of the first in the country specialise in central heating before the boom of the 1960s; one of the first customers was Alderman Snowman the Mayor of Hampstead who celebrated his wedding anniversary by having central heating installed in his home as a surprise for his wife.

The firm's founder had been brought up by his grandparents after his father had died when he was two. Brian's grandparents owned the firm of Garner & Son builders and Brian started his own business from his own home and from Garner & Son's yard at the bottom of his grandparents' garden.

In those early days Grace Broadhurst, Brian's wife, did the paperwork and took the phone calls in and amongst caring for their children. The couple had

Top: *Oak Day Unit, Tolworth Hospital.*
Above left: *The main boiler room at Tolworth Hospital.*

four children, Nigel, Debra, Sarah and Andrew, although only Nigel would eventually join his father in the business.

Needing to move his equipment around, Brian paid £250 for a van and, lacking any more money to invest, borrowed large tools when he needed them. At the time he only had £240 so had to borrow the other £10 to buy the van.

The first contract job at Multisprings Bedding factory in Mitcham paid £100 - for labour only - although Brian's first wage packet came to just £8. It was hardly rich pickings.

But things improved. Brian Broadhurst's first employees were David Garner who had worked on Brian's first factory contract, Alan Lucas, an old school friend and Harry Wheeler, who has since moved to Australia.

Business may have improved but other problems remained to be resolved. Brian bought Garner's yard from his Uncle Don who had been left it by his grandmother. Two years later Brian bought his grandparents' old house too and moved his office there, but disaster struck when Brian could not prove to the authorities that the yard had always been there. Unable to provide the necessary evidence of

'ancient rights' and unmoved by Brian's threat to move back the pigs which had once been kept there, new premises were needed.

Eventually, in 1974, Brian bought a bungalow and yard where in 1976 the present offices in Red Lion Road Surbiton were built. During that first scorching hot summer Brian would cool himself off in a 200 gallon tank of water - Brian built the new offices himself in just six weeks with one brick layer, Ronnie Tandy. In 1980 a top floor was added. Graham Fisher, one of the firm's present directors, began his career with the business as a pipe fitter in 1972. When Brian took the six weeks off to build the new offices Graham was brought into the office to run the firm and was then made a director in 1989 when the firm became limited.

The current management team comprises the chairman Brian Broadhurst, Graham Fisher as managing director with Nigel Broadhurst as a director and Brian Groves as supervisor.

The firm has had many long standing employees: pipe-fitters Bob Sykes, Colin Groombridge, Micky

In 1974, Brian bought the site where the present Red Lion Road premises were built

Below: *Addleston Day Centre.*

Platts, Tony Whitehead, John Nutley, Pete Moss and Micky Garner - and in the office too, Sylvia Lipscombe who spent 28 years with the firm as Brian Broadhurst's personal secretary before her retirement in 2000. The firm's 28 staff now use 12 vans and cover most of London although they have done jobs as far afield as Cambridge and Ffestiniog.

Amongst the many interesting jobs undertaken by the company have been the installation of heating and air conditioning in buildings for Grosvenor Estate in Buckingham Palace Road, a new heating plant in the Guild Hall as well as work at Kingston, Tolworth and Surbiton hospitals.

Brian Broadhurst is now retired, spending his time gardening, tending Koi carp and golfing. We have much to thank the Brian Broadhursts of the world

for. Not too long ago we would wake on winter mornings to see frost flowers growing on our window panes; we would get out of bed and cautiously feel with our toes for our slippers and, if we failed, we would feel the icy touch of winter make our feet tingle when they hit linoleum instead of the rug or the slippers we had hoped to find. How many of us remember rooms which we didn't even use in our homes during the winter months except perhaps on Sundays when our mothers may have lit a fire in the grate in honour of visitors.

What the Romans started in their crude though effective way Broadhurst Heating Ltd has helped develop over the decades into a fine art. Today's highly efficient and effective heating and environmental systems have opened up every room in our homes to us all the year round and enabled us to discard those multiple layers of clothing which were once so essential everywhere except for right in front of the fire. Yes, they were happy times huddled around the wireless or television but how many of us would choose to turn the clock back and do without central heating, a luxury which has now become an essential part of everyday living?

Left: Broadhurst's premises today.
Top: An old people's home in Walton on Thames.

On the road again

How many times have we watched huge mysterious loads being transported on our roads and wondered just how the drivers manage to negotiate our crowded highways? In the past, though our roads may have been less crowded, they were invariably far narrower and the driver's job was much more difficult. Amongst the few firms which began making such difficult deliveries decades ago are Kingston's Adams & Adams Ltd and Graham Adams Ltd.

Adams & Adams Ltd, now largely involved in warehousing, was formed in 1943; the firm's current main business activities include machinery handling and storage together with the running of its offices and an industrial estate.

The associated firm of Graham Adams Ltd was formed as a limited company in 1954 to carry on the business of haulage contractors, specialising in the removal and relocation of engineering equipment; it is undoubtedly one of the oldest remaining family firms in Britain specialising in complete factory relocations.

Both companies have been associated with the transport industry since 1926 when two brothers Alfred and Arthur Adams, known as Ben and Joe, formed Adams Bros (Super Transport) Ltd with capital of just £85 loaned by their mother.

Until starting their own business the brothers had worked for George Bristow, builders merchants and hauliers, before buying their own lorry carrying anything they could. During the general strike they even put seats in their lorries and bussed people into central London.

Helped by their mother, the brothers' young firm began life operating from their home in Cowley Road, Kingston and from a yard in Elton Road. Joe drove whilst Ben ran the office. The yard at Elton Road was used until 1935 when the firm moved to its present location in Dickerage Lane, New Malden.

Above: *The original land in the 1930s.*
Below: *Joe (left) and Ben with the first Bluebird to be taken abroad in 1937.*

The following year 26 vehicles and 11 trailers belonging to Adams Brothers were nationalised leaving only Adams & Adams and George Bristow in family hands.

With denationalisation in 1954 Graham Adams was formed to operate the fleet of vehicles. Graham, Ben's son, would take control of the new company following his demobilisation from the Royal Army Service Corps. The first purchases were four Commer seven tonners.

The firm continued to specialise in heavy haulage, carrying boats and machinery, and soon had 27 trucks and 120 staff between the various companies.

In the following years the company diversified into property development, culminating in the building of the firm's present headquarters, Adams House in 1961, to which an extra floor was added some ten years later.

The founder, Ben Adams died in 1997 aged 92; subsequently the Adams & Adams company has developed more warehousing and storage with less emphasis on transport.

Today's directors include Graham Adams who is chairman and managing director and his sister, Sylvia Selfe, whilst Graham's daughter, Marion Adams, who joined the firm part time in 1990 is now both a director and company secretary running the firm on the day-to-day basis advised by her father. Has £85 ever been better invested, we wonder?

The 1930s saw the company involved with the famous Campbell family of car and boat racing enthusiasts, transporting both their cars and boats - an Adams' vehicle becoming the first articulated lorry to cross the channel when it took the Bluebird speedboat to Switzerland. The firm took Sir Malcolm Campbell's boat abroad twice in the 1930s. In 1937 the speedboat was transported to Locarno and in 1938 to Geneva and Bristenberg for successful attempts to gain the water speed record of over 130 mph. Carrying such a tricky load over 1,200 miles of continental and alpine roads in those pre-motorway days was no joke but the firm was up to the task. Donald Campbell eventually became a director of the company.

In 1945 the brothers bought out the business of their old employer George Bristow but two years later the firm split in two. The firm of Adams Brothers (Super Transport) Ltd went to Joe whilst Adams & Adams went to Ben: who got which was decided on the toss of a coin.

Above: Loading equipment preparing for a factory removal. Top: An Adams vehicle lifting a World War II bomb in New Malden. Right: The premises in 1961.

A shopping paradise

Eden Walk Shopping Centre was the first shopping centre in Kingston and one of the very first such centres in the whole country. Situated in the heart of the town Eden Walk started Kingston off as the great retail centre it has become today. The Centre is still an integral part of the town, providing a home to some of the biggest names in retailing. The multi-storey car park providing 725 parking places right in the town centre also hosts the council's Shopmobility Scheme giving full access to the town for the disabled and elderly.

The Centre was built in three phases, starting in 1964-66 with the northern parade of shops (Sainsburys, Habitat and Marks & Spencers) in Eden Walk and the multi-storey car park. That first development created Eden Walk as a thoroughfare for shoppers and provided access to the car park from Eden Street.

The second phase (BHS and Millennium House) was developed more than ten years later between 1977 and 1979 taking the entrance to the car park into Union Street via the present spiral ramp. Eden Walk was also extended through to Union Street giving shoppers greater access to the old town. The new Alderman Judge mall was also created, being named after eminent local politician and Justice of the Peace, CE Judge. BHS was built over what was once Brady's Arcade.

The final phase in 1984 saw the building of the Boots store, the shops along its southern wall and the creation of the Cloisters when Pratt's Passage was repositioned to allow for the extension of M&S. The Princess Royal, Princess Anne, visited the centre for the opening ceremony.

Many younger residents of Kingston may however wonder what was here before Eden Walk. There have certainly been buildings there for a very long time indeed, far, far beyond the memory or even the oldest inhabitant of the town. When the first phase was begun archaeologists uncovered artefacts from the Saxon era. The Centre was in fact built on what were once the grounds of Warwick Castle; the actual site of which being the immediate neighbours at 53 and 54 Eden Street.

Above: *The multi-storey car park.*
Below: *Eden Walk from the Centre Square.*

buildings coming and going over the passing years.

The Compasses public house for example, demolished in 1977 for the second phase, was situated opposite the old Post Office and was recorded on maps of the area at the beginning of the 19th century - although at that time the Post Office was a Bridewell Prison. Next door but one to the Compasses was a passageway that led to Young's Buildings, then on to Pratt's Passage. Young's Buildings were roughly situated on what is now the centre square.

Eden Street was originally called Heathen Street and has been part of Kingston since the 13th century. The name was only changed to pander to Victorian sensibilities: no doubt Kingston's stern Victorian churchgoers felt more than a little satisfaction at seeing such a wicked and ungodly name disappear to be replaced by one with self evident biblical connotations. The distinctive crescent shape of the street was originally created simply because of marshland which it once skirted. As the marsh was drained the area began to throng with shops and works, continuing to the present day, with many different

The Boots building has been built on what was previously the print works which at one time wrapped itself around the memorial gardens on which there was once a briefly used cemetery. The local map of 1813 does not show any church or burial ground on the site, however by 1865 a closed cemetery is marked there. The print works were built on the site between 1913 and 1932 prior to which there had been several shops located there. Brady's Arcade was built some time after 1932 when it became home to ten small lock-up shops.

Each Saturday some 30,000 visitors in 1,600 cars now visit the Eden Centre's 28 shop units. Most will have one thing on their minds: shopping. But perhaps a few will now spare a thought for what the shopping centre also represents: the latest baton bearer in Kingston's relay race through history.

Top: *The Centre Square is a popular venue for many events. Here is Kingston University Youth Band.*
Above: *Eden Walk from Eden Street.*

A life of learning

Education, education, education: that oft-repeated political priority has long been at the centre of people's thoughts in Kingston. Kingston University is a particular source of local pride having gone from strength to strength since its creation and is now one of the top universities in the country. The university's success has been widely reported in national newspaper league tables, helping make it the higher educational institute of first choice for thousands of new students each year.

In 1999, the Royal Borough of Kingston Upon Thames celebrated the hundredth anniversary of the founding of The Kingston Technical Institute which had opened on 11th February 1899; it is to that institution that both Kingston University and Kingston College owe their common origin.

Kingston University began life, however, only in 1992, having previously been Kingston Polytechnic. In the 1990s, initially as a polytechnic and later as the University, Kingston awarded well in excess of 40,000 higher education qualifications; its student population almost doubling during the period and its financial turnover rising by 100 per cent from just under £40 million in 1990 to over £80 million by the end of the millennium.

Due to the relatively simple change of title to that of a University in 1992, Kingston was in the first batch of polytechnics to attain university status; an inauguration ceremony was held in All Saints' Church on 24th June, which followed an academic procession from the Guildhall.

The mid 1990s saw many developments to the university's property. The lease on the former Hawker aircraft factory at Canbury Park, where technology and sculpture students were taught, expired and, in 1993, a

Above: *The academic procession returning to the Guildhall, following the Inauguration Ceremony of the University on 24 June 1992.* ***Below:*** *Kingston University's fashion students are world renowned.*

proposal was put forward to move the School of Mechanical, Aeronautical and Production Engineering to the former Smith's Industries' factory site in Roehampton Vale. The building was opened, refurbished and fully occupied in October 1993 and, in May the following year, the remaining technology students moved into the new Sopwith building in Fassett Road.

The University also received two major gifts of property: firstly Dorich House the former home of sculptor Dora Gordine and her husband, the Honourable Richard Hare; in addition the Stanley Picker Trust generously bequeathed a new art gallery as part of the Middle Mill development. In terms of property, however, it was the second half of the decade which saw the largest project, completed in 1997: the redevelopment of the Kingston Hill campus.

Sir Frank Lampl, Chairman of the Bovis Construction Group, became Kingston University's inaugural Chancellor in June 1994 at a ceremony held in the Great Hall at Hampton Court Palace.

The following year saw the establishment of a new faculty of healthcare sciences - a joint venture with St George's Hospital Medical School. Initially, 800 nursing and midwifery students transferred from a former NHS college as the higher education sector became increasingly responsible for the provision of healthcare qualifications.

On 31st December 1997, Vice-Chancellor Bob Smith retired. His successes over a 15-year reign had been impressive; the most visible perhaps being the large rise in students, from 5,800 on his arrival in 1982, to 15,000 on his departure. Peter Scott, a former editor of the Times Higher Education Supplement and Pro Vice-Chancellor (External Affairs) of Leeds University, took over the mantle in January 1998.

Since its creation, Kingston University has grown into a nationally and internationally acclaimed institute. Its teaching reputation speaks for itself through excellent Government assessment results and national league tables. In September 2000, The Sunday Times shortlisted Kingston for its 'University of the Year Award', saying 'students should be breaking the doors down to get in'.

Areas of particular strength include design and aeronautical engineering. Kingston's fashion design graduates, for example, are employed by world famous fashion houses such as Georgio Armani, Hugo Boss and Calvin Klein. One of the notable triumphs for the university came in late 1999 when the university acquired a Merlin 520-T flight simulator for its aeronautical engineers, the first and one of only two universities in the country to provide such a facility for its students.

In many sporting areas too, Kingston University students are beginning to make a name for themselves, competing at local, regional, national and even international levels. One example is Kingston University Sportswoman of the Year Helena Malenczuk, who gained silver and bronze in two European Championships for rowing.

Today, tens of thousands of former students can look back with fond memories of Kingston University, the place where they received that most priceless of gifts: their education.

Above left: In the 1990s the University acquired a Merlin 520-T flight simulator for use by its aero-engineers. Above right: The Stanley Picker Gallery, a public art facility bequeathed by the Stanley Picker Trust. Below: Kingston University rowers compete internationally.

Acknowledgments

The Kingston Museum and Heritage Service

Tim Everson - Local History Officer

Jill Lamb - Archivist

Thanks are also due to
Judith Dennis and Andrew Mitchell who penned the editorial text
and Steve Ainsworth for his copywriting skills

CONTENTS

ENGLISH HERITAGE

INTRODUCTION

Little angels or little devils – this book presents a selection of professionally taken photographs of children from the 1870s to the 1950s, capturing them at work or play, posed or seemingly unaware of the camera. Such photographs do more than record a collection of people and places,they provide reflections of something we have all experienced. Whether we view them as artistic works or as sources of information on ages past, we will probably all find at least one image here that encapsulates our own view of childhood or provokes a vivid memory from our own past.

Photography rapidly replaced painting as a means of recording people and events, and by the 1860s there were photographers' studios in most towns as well as travelling photographers who recorded local communities and events. Though photographs were expensive they became accessible to far more people than paintings had ever been. It became common for portraits to be taken to mark important family events such as weddings and christenings, or to mark milestones in children's lives such as a boy's first pair of breeches or a girl putting up her hair.

Photographers have to please their customers and consciously or unconsciously they reflect the values and attitudes of the age. Middle- and upper-class Victorian and Edwardian children were carefully posed with suitable props, often toys, and dressed to emphasise their innocence and purity. There was a fashion for showing them as docile 'little angels'; some photographers' handbooks of the time even included instructions on how to attach angel's wings. This attitude to children and childhood may appear sentimental today but this trend was no doubt influenced by the much higher rate of child deaths in the Victorian era. Some children were photographed prior to being buried, possibly the only record left to their parents.

These photographs reveal many curious details about life in the past. For example, Victorian and Edwardian children's clothing for both rich and poor was evidently a scaled-down version of adult attire rather than specifically designed for them. Many photographs were obviously posed, such as the picture of the two boys making a haystack in what look to be their best clothes. In contrast, poorer children were often photographed more naturally, outside playing with their friends for example, wearing a wide variety of often ill-fitting clothes and footwear clearly passed down from older or richer children. The extreme poverty and deprivation of some children is all too evident.

Children were not always viewed as innocents, however. The middle-class view that poorer children were untamed creatures needing firm control to curb their innate lack of morals, is reflected in a different style of photography used to record the working classes. One photograph, which includes both rich and poor, shows the village children paddling with clothes tucked up while their more modestly attired and better dressed companions look on from the river bank.

This bucolic scene was at odds from the reality for many children. Working class children had to earn a living from an early age and photography has captured this too. Rural children are pictured working in agriculture and as domestic servants, while those from the towns are employed packing tea or making marmalade. The shocking image of a pit disaster memorial (page 111) is a telling insight into the lives of working children and also into the different attitudes to boys and girls.

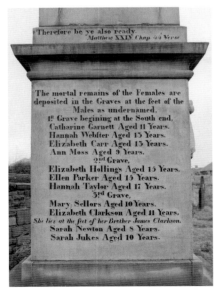

It was not until the 1870 Education Act that provision was made for all children to receive elementary schooling, though this was not fully enforced until education became free in 1891. The school leaving age in 1899 was 11 rising to 14 in 1918. The Victorian school groups captured in this collection often show a wide age range and are sometimes shown in front of severe looking school buildings with high walls and windows to keep the children in – and all possible distractions out.

As the formality of the Victorian and Edwardian ages gave way to more relaxed attitudes, photography became less of a novelty and improved technology meant its subjects no longer had to stand stock still while the photograph was taken. Hence from the 1920s photographs show people looking far more relaxed and natural. Photographs show children engrossed in their own world, seemingly unaware of the camera. Images from the 1940s and 1950s show many children dressed very formally by today's standards although the changes that became obvious in the 1960s are beginning to appear.

The major theme for these images of childhood is play. With most of the images dating from a time before all households had a television, let alone a computer, the emphasis is very much on do-it-yourself games: children skipping, climbing trees, messing about in water, making daisy chains, sailing boats and playing leapfrog. There is an overall sense of carefree, undirected days, though on closer inspection there is evidence that some children had much shorter and less enjoyable childhoods than others. Older children can be seen in charge of younger siblings and adults sometimes appear in a supervisory or even suspicious role. In one scene, young children with hair cropped to deter lice stand looking forlorn outside a public house 'waiting for father', a standard theme of Victorian morals (page 26).

Above all, this wonderful collection includes some timeless childhood moments that will resonate with many people: two boys totally absorbed in the careful placing of a stone, a little girl staring intently at a desired cake in the shop window, a wet woolly swimsuit flapping around the knees, a boring wait outside the shop.

Mary Mills

*"**B**IRTHS deaths and marriages were really important to a small community. If there was a baby born everybody was thrilled to bits and went to see it."*

A portrait of the Franklin children
at Hellidon, Northamptonshire.
Alfred Newton & Son *1900*

A young child looking
over its mother's shoulder.
John Gay *1946-1980*

A young boy in a sailor suit,
Fawsley, Northamptonshire.
Alfred Newton & Son *1901*

A baby crying in his pram.
John Gay *1954*

A small child sits bareback on a
pony in Snitterfield, Warwickshire.
Alfred Newton & Son *1896-1920*

A young girl sitting on a wheeled
horse in a garden in Warwickshire.
Alfred Newton & Son *1896-1920*

Mrs Franklin's children,
Hellidon, Northamptonshire.
Alfred Newton & Son *July 1902*

A young boy and his dog outside
Ivy Cottage in Marsh Gibbon,
Buckinghamshire.
Alfred Newton & Son *1904*

A young child peering out of a pram in a London park.
John Gay *1950-1970*

A girl holding her doll, Upper Boddington, Northamptonshire.
Alfred Newton & Son *1896-1920*

"*FRIDAY night was bath night. We would have the copper going to heat the water. The bath would come out in front of the fire and we all used the same water. On cold winter nights mother would take the hot shelf out of the oven, wrap it in a harding apron and put it in our bed. It was lovely.*"

18

Six of Mr Turvey's children. George Turvey was shopkeeper and sub-postmaster at Preston Bissett, Buckinghamshire.
Alfred Newton & Son *1904*

The nursery in Minley Manor, Hawley, Hampshire. A young girl nurses her doll while her small brother or sister sleeps next to her.
Bedford Lemere *Date unknown*

Two boys, possibly the Wareing
brothers, leading horses at Leam
House, Hellidon, Northamptonshire.
Alfred Newton & Son *1901*

Three children with their
pets outside their house
in Northamptonshire.
Alfred Newton & Son *1896-1920*

A mother reading to her children and the family dog, Great Munden, Hertfordshire.
John Gay *1957*

A nanny with two charges at Staverton, Northamptonshire.
Alfred Newton & Son *1896-1920*

Mrs Alliband's (or Allibone's)
children at the front door
of their house in Hellidon,
Northamptonshire.
Alfred Newton & Son *1901*

Standing on tiptoes to reach
the sink in Mrs Tinsley's
kitchen. A prefab in Lyham
Road, London.
Photographer unknown
22 September 1945

Children wait outside a
public house in London.
Campbell's Press Studio

Buying ice cream on a
sunny day at Clissold Park,
Stoke Newington, London.
John Gay *1964*

27

Playing outside courtyard
housing in Bowling Green,
Warwick, Warwickshire.
Photographer unknown *1946*

Standing in a panelled doorway
in North Lees Hall, Derbyshire.
J A Gotch *15 August 1900*

"*Our young days were better because we never knew anyone who was stand-offish and we were all in the same boat.*"

Three friends in Kentish Town, London.
John Gay *1946-1970*

A group of children on the village
green in Hellidon, Northamptonshire.
Alfred Newton & Son *1901*

Children in a lane at Dinton,
Buckinghamshire.
Alfred Newton & Son *1904*

Children sitting on steps near
the harbour at Newlyn, Cornwall.
Alfred Newton & Son *1907*

Posing for the camera in front of
King Alfred's statue, Winchester,
Hampshire.
W A Clarke *Date unknown*

Children playing in a derelict house
in Hellidon, Northamptonshire.
Alfred Newton & Son *1896-1920*

'Miss Russell' and her companions,
Avon Dassett, Warwickshire.
Alfred Newton & Son *July 1902*

A group of children near a
refreshment stall in St James's
Park, Westminster, London.
York & Son *1870-1900*

A group of village children pose
for the camera in Preston Bissett,
Buckinghamshire.
Alfred Newton & Son *1904*

A group of children from
Hellidon, Northamptonshire.
Alfred Newton & Son *July 1902*

Children dressed in smocks from
the village of Hethe, Oxfordshire.
Alfred Newton & Son *July 1901*

"We used to go to the seaside once a year on buses or by train. We used to take a penny a week to school and save up for the trip. It cost ⅓d. We couldn't afford to go away for a week. We used to play on the sands because we had no money for anything else."

A little boy and a dog look
like unwilling participants
in a shopping trip in Padstow,
Cornwall.
John Gay *1946-1959*

Boys play in the boating pool
at New Brighton, Merseyside.
Photographer unknown
August 1930

47

A woman photographs her son
at the Peter Pan statue in Hyde
Park, London.
John Gay *1960-1970*

Children ride a 'Big Wheel' on
Great Yarmouth beach, Norfolk,
as their mothers look on.
Hallam Ashley *26 July 1947*

Children paddle in a sheep
washing pool on a hot summer's
day at Cowley, Oxfordshire.
Henry Taunt *Early 20th century*

A little girl and her dog have their photograph taken with the sentry at Horse Guards, Whitehall, London.
John Gay *1952-1970*

A group of friends are photographed with a policeman outside Buckingham Palace, London.
John Gay *1950-1970*

A Girl Guide receives a Fortitude Badge
from Lady Baden-Powell at a Guide and
Scout Rally at Keswick Park, Norfolk.
Hallam Ashley *13 July 1951*

Girl Guides huddle around a
small camp fire to keep warm
at Keswick Park, Norfolk.
Hallam Ashley *13 May 1951*

A young girl looks longingly at the display at Clare Cake Shop in Padstow, Cornwall.
John Gay *1946-1959*

Two young children exploring the shore on the South Cornish coast.
John Gay *1946-1959*

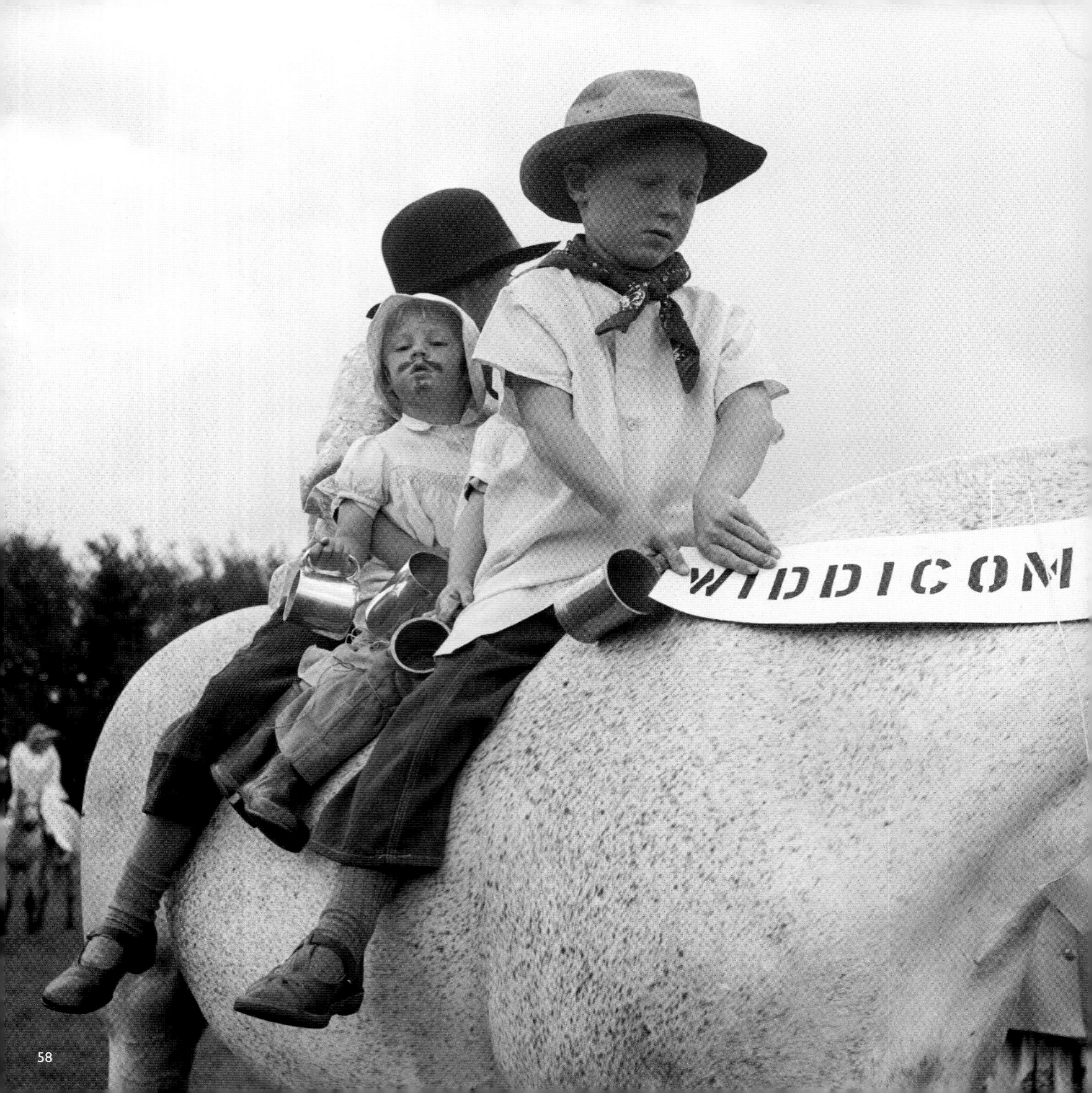
WIDDICOM

A fancy dress competition at
Creech St Michael, Somerset.
John Gay *1946-1960*

Four friends take a donkey ride
on Bridlington Beach under the
supervision of the proprietor.
Hallam Ashley *September 1959*

"*AT playtime the boys played football, cricket, marbles, whip and top and leapfrog. Girls played hopscotch, skipping, shuttlecock, whilst tig and picketball could be played together. We played piesball, a version of rounders but we used our hands instead of a bat. If any of the boys caught up with a girl while she was running for the corners, they took a kiss. I was a good runner and never got caught.*"

A boy stands proudly with his
bicycle as other children look
on, Scawby, North Lincolnshire.
Alfred Newton & Son *July 1902*

Children at Great Munden,
Hertfordshire, one of whom
is poking his tongue out at
the camera.
John Gay *1963*

Paddling in the River Thames
near Tower Pier, London.
S W Rawlings *1945-1965*

A young girl tries to reach
the drinking fountain in
Clissold Park, London.
John Gay *1960-1980*

A young girl leads a goat and cart
in Towcester, Northamptonshire.
Alfred Newton & Son *April 1904*

Boys play in a handcart near
Club Row Markets, London, as
a smartly dressed boy walks past.
John Gay *1960-1969*

67

Harrods Toy Department,
Knightsbridge, London.
Bedford Lemere *1919*

Girls play with a rope tied
round a lamp post, London.
John Gay *1952-1953*

A group of girls dressed as
'The Gipsies' outside Charwelton
School, Northamptonshire.
Alfred Newton & Son *1896-1920*

"THE GIPSIES"
CHARWELTON SCHOOL

Young children in fancy dress
at Hellidon, Northamptonshire.
Alfred Newton & Son *1896-1920*

Children having fun sledging
down a country lane in Halifax,
Yorkshire.
John Gay *1962-1978*

Children play on a slide outside
a post war housing development
in Streatham, London.
Eric de Maré *1945-1980*

Sailing a yacht on a boating pond,
London.
John Gay *1950-1980*

Boys pull a rowing boat to shore
at Robin Hood's Bay, Yorkshire.
Hallam Ashley *2 July 1954*

A boy pokes his head
through the roof of the
Butter Cross in Witney,
Oxfordshire.
Henry Taunt *1860-1922*

A girl and boy stand proudly
beside their home-made
doll's house, Warwickshire.
Alfred Newton & Son
1896-1920

A cricket match in the
village of Reeth, Yorkshire.
Hallam Ashley *17 May 1950*

A selection of children's toys
in the British Pavilion at the
Paris Exhibition.
**From the Millar and Harris
Collection** *6 July 1937*

Boys dressed as Native Americans,
Hellidon, Northamptonshire.
Alfred Newton & Son *1896-1920*

Climbing the old tree by
the village pond in Aldbury,
Hertfordshire.
John Gay *1946-1959*

Playing with toys in Great
Ormond Street Hospital
for Sick Children, London.
Bedford Lemere *1894*

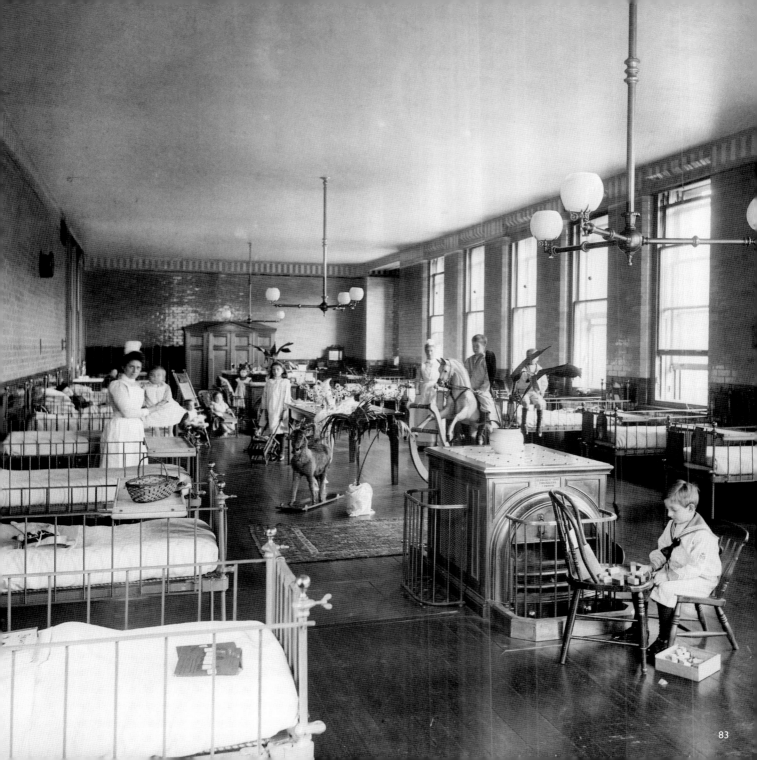

A boy and girl with a hoop and stick, East Hagbourne, Oxfordshire. **Photographer and date unknown**

Children play with toys on the doorstep of a house in Sandwich, Kent. **John Gay** *1954*

"*AT infant school they used to put us to bed for a nap in the afternoon on foldaway beds. We used to have tea at school — two slices of jam and bread and a pint of cocoa. We had that for breakfast too.*"

School children and their teacher stand outside their school house at Freeland, Oxfordshire. The priest and well dressed ladies could possibly be school governors.
Henry Taunt *1900*

A nursery group play in an Islington square, London.
John Gay *1946-1959*

Children play percussion instruments
at the Highgate Society Children's
Playgroup, London.
John Gay *1965-1975*

Pupils at the Royal Military Asylum in
Chelsea, London, lined up in front of the
building in uniform. It was built for the
children of soldiers in the regular army.
York & Son *1870-1900*

THE ROYAL MILITARY ASYLUM FOR THE CHILDREN OF SOLDIERS OF THE REGULAR ARMY

A gym class at
John Roan School,
Greenwich, London.
S W Newbery *c1926*

Drawing at a table with
coloured pencils, Suffolk.
John Gay *1946-1959*

Children at Badby School,
Northamptonshire, hold a
cheery message as two stern
school mistresses look on.
Alfred Newton & Son *1896-1920*

"WE'D go wassailing at Christmas, 'Mumming' they called it. We'd get dressed up and black our faces. No-one could pick out my mother because she used to get dressed up as a man. On Whit Sunday everything was new, you couldn't go to chapel if all your clothes weren't new."

Children posing with May Day
garlands, Oxfordshire.
Henry Taunt *1860-1922*

A boy admires the nativity crib
at St Peter Mancroft Church,
Norwich, Norfolk.
Hallam Ashley *1952*

Girls at East Hanney,
Oxfordshire, pose before
the Maypole dancing begins.
Frederick Ault *1860-1914*

A group portrait of men and boys
holding willow sticks to beat the
bounds at Cowley, Oxfordshire.
Henry Taunt *1914*

Boys scramble for coins during
a beating the bounds ceremony
at Oxford, Oxfordshire.
Henry Taunt *1908*

The Queen of the Chipping
Camden Floral Festival is
surrounded by pageboys
and girls dressed in white.
Henry Taunt *1897*

Three young bridesmaids
wait outside a church.
John Gay *1950-1959*

104

"*I* WENT *into service at 14. My mother thought there would be better living conditions than in the mills. I got ten shillings a week and my keep but I didn't see any of it. I was allowed to see sixpence and send the rest home. I used to get one afternoon off a week.*"

A boy working as a gardener
at Hellidon, Northamptonshire.
Alfred Newton & Son *October 1903*

The Lloyd family of Great Dixter in
East Sussex haymaking with the help
of some of the convalescing soldiers
who were billeted at the house during
World War I.
Nathaniel Lloyd *July 1916*

A girl at her spinning machine at the Early Blanket Factory, Witney, Oxfordshire.
Henry Taunt *1890*

The Huskar Pit Disaster Memorial showing the names of the children who were drowned whilst working in the pit when it flooded. The public outcry that followed caused Parliament to prohibit boys under 10 years and all girls from working underground. Silkstone, South Yorkshire.
Bob Skingle *November 1993*

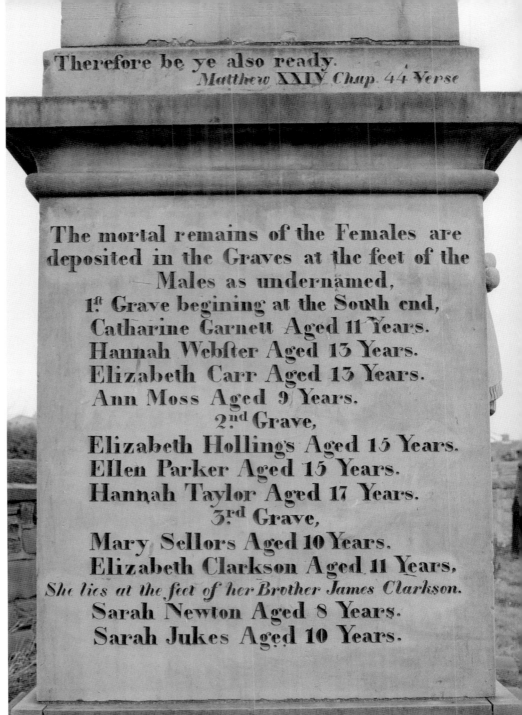

Therefore be ye also ready.
Matthew XXIV Chap. 44 Verse

The mortal remains of the Females are deposited in the Graves at the feet of the — Males as undernamed,
1ᵗ Grave begining at the South end,
Catharine Garnett Aged 11 Years.
Hannah Webſter Aged 13 Years.
Elizabeth Carr Aged 13 Years.
Ann Moss Aged 9 Years.
2ⁿᵈ Grave,
Elizabeth Hollings Aged 15 Years.
Ellen Parker Aged 15 Years.
Hannah Taylor Aged 17 Years.
3ʳᵈ Grave,
Mary Sellors Aged 10 Years.
Elizabeth Clarkson Aged 11 Years,
She lies at the feet of her Brother James Clarkson.
Sarah Newton Aged 8 Years.
Sarah Jukes Aged 10 Years.

Young boys label tins of tea whilst
being watched by a foreman at
Butler's Wharf, London.
Photographer unknown *c1910*

Two smartly dressed boys build
a thatched haystack at Byfield,
Northamptonshire.
Alfred Newton & Son *1904*

113

Young girls in the Waring & Gillow
factory in Lancaster during
World War I, making up wooden
boxes possibly for munitions.
Bedford Lemere *1917*

National Monuments Record

The photographs in this book all come from the collections of the National Monuments Record (NMR).

The NMR is one of the largest publicly accessible archives in Britain and is the biggest dedicated to the historic environment. It is an unparalleled collection of images, old and new, which has been growing for over 60 years.

Set up as the National Buildings Record (NBR) in 1941 in response to the threat to historic buildings from aerial bombardment during World War II, it immediately began its own recording programme as well as collecting historic negatives and prints.

In 1963 it came under the auspices of the Royal Commission on the Historical Monuments of England and in 1999 was transferred to English Heritage. Today the collection comprises more than eight million photographs and other archive items relating to England's architecture and archaeology.

It continues to accept major collections of national importance and is a repository for material created by English Heritage's staff photographers. The collection may be consulted at the National Monuments Record office in Swindon.

Telephone 01793 414600 or email nmrinfo@english-heritage.org.uk for details.

www.english-heritage.org.uk/viewfinder

If you would like enlargements of photographs in this book please call enquiries on 01793 414600 quoting the reference numbers below.

Page 6	AA97/05337	41	AA97/05318	77	BB98/02520
7	AA054104	42	AA97/05427	78	AA98/09827
8	BB98/10803	43	AA97/05222	80	CC013950
9	AA054090	46	AA054083	81	BB98/10578
10	BB97/08254	47	CC80/00454	82	AA054084
11	BB97/08145	48	AA054111	83	BL/12177
12	AA97/05927	49	AA98/16596	84	BB91/11268
13	AA97/07429	50	CC71/00076	85	AA054088
14	AA054110	52	AA054108	88	CC73/01085
15	BB98/02504	53	AA054109	89	AA054048
18	AA97/05249	54	AA98/16109	90	AA054099
19	BB86/00795	55	AA99/02429	91	CC97/00178
20	AA97/05948	56	AA054082	92	BB032627
21	BB98/10766	57	AA04080	94	AA054081
22	AA054089	58	AA054095	95	BB98/01626
23	BB98/01901	59	AA99/02370	98	CC72/00168
24	AA97/05429	62	AA97/05919	99	AA99/02431
25	MOW H49/7	63	AA054092	100	CC72/00178
26	BB73/07074	64	AA001173	102	CC73/00553
27	AA054107	65	AA054106	103	CC72/02365
28	AA48/02779	66	AA97/06002	104	CC73/00602
29	BB44/00683	67	AA054101	105	AA054085
32	AA054103	68	BL/24450/05	108	BB98/06048
33	AA97/05428	69	AA054102	109	CC002585
34	AA97/07509	70	BB98/05909	110	CC73/00946
35	AA97/07540	71	BB98/02481	111	AA93/01061
36	AA50/09458	72	AA054098	112	BB87/09690
37	BB98/02389	73	AA98/06311	113	BB97/08360
38	AA97/08022	74	AA054079	114	BL/23741/15
39	AA97/05319	75	AA98/09806		
40	CC97/00268	76	CC48/00150		